Cat Tales

True Love Stories

Dr. Sharon Eisen

&

Linda Francese

To order additional copies of this book, contact:
Xlibris Corporation
1-888-795-4274
www.Xlibris.com
Orders@Xlibris.com
67541

Contents

Dedication

This book is dedicated to Bentley a.k.a. Bravo Bentley, his registered name; the purple kitty to his fans in the show hall; Benty at the clinic; and Benty Eisen to his family.

To Betamax Francese a.k.a. Beta to his friends and family, or BeeyaB, the name given to him when my son Johnny was eighteen months old, and stuck as BetaB.

And to the cats that are special in your life, the cats that don't have a home, the cats that don't get a story written about them in a book. Because every cat has a story, every cat has a tale.

Foreword

Without a doubt, Sharon Eisen and Linda Francese are two of the cattiest people we know . . . but of course, we mean this in the kindest and most complimentary way! As these two dedicated and delightful women have cared for our cats over the years, we have come to know them as compassionate people who are equally fluent in the language of feline medicine and the language of feline-human relationships. They have been there for our cats, and for us, through difficult health issues and also shared with us the exhilaration and joy of bringing a new kitty into our home.

The tales in this book represent a sampling of the many experiences that Sharon and Linda have shared, or heard about, through their clients. They will warm your heart, make you laugh, perhaps shed a tear, but mostly, remind you what an amazing animal is that creature we know as cat.

Jean Cocteau wrote, "I love cats because I enjoy my home; and little by little, they become its visible soul."

Fellow cat lovers, we know you will enjoy each of these tales as much as we have.

Florence and Wendell Minor

Failure Is Impossible

The cat leapt up, but
That very split second the windowsill
Moved
Slightly, out of reach
The cat, twisting in air, chose the floor
Instead, and landing
Began combing his fur
With his teeth
Then lifting his leg
He licked underneath
And between
Thoroughly
Sniffed a stray speck
Redid his right paw
All the time in the world
Secured
He padded off
Nonchalant, insouciant
Tail erect
Dignity intact
The play complete

—Helen Eisen, 2007

Introduction

Cats are the number 1 companion animal, with an estimated ninety million pet cats in the United States today. As a nation, we find cats beautiful, interesting, and funny. We spend lots of money on them, spoil them, and often let them run our lives. We enjoy coming home to and caring for our cats; many of us even like to sleep with them. Right now, in millions of bedrooms across the country, you will likely find cats curled up on pillows and snuggled up under blankets. We miss our cats so much when we go on vacation that many hotels have taken to offering guests a "loaner cat" for the duration of their stay.

For the past twenty-four years, Dr. Sharon Eisen has been a practicing veterinarian specializing in cats. She has cared for thousands of them and has heard literally hundreds of cat tales.

When Linda Francese joined the team, she too began to collect these incredible tales. Although owners bring their cats in for medical care, visits to the clinic often end with colorful stories that go way beyond the medical issues that brought them in. Some cat tales are medical miracles, like the cat that fell from a seven-story building and survived. Some showcase cats' amazing skills, like the one about the cat that found its way home after being abandoned thirty miles away. Still others are about cats that have helped their owners get through traumatic times.

Cats share our journeys and become part of our personal histories. They help us document the milestones in our lives. We often hear things like, "My cat came into my life just as I was getting divorced," or "We adopted her from the shelter when our first son was born." They comfort us during times of illness and distress. They move to new homes with us. They may even travel with us to faraway places and grow old with us.

These are not tales about famous cats, nor are they tales told by famous people. They are true stories told by people who come to the office or whom we meet in other settings. When Dr. Eisen mentions that she is a cat veterinarian or Linda a technician, the stories begin. "Let me tell you about my cat" and "Do you want to hear an unbelievable story about this cat" or "Have you ever heard of a cat like this?" On airplanes, in shopping malls, and at parties, we hear cat tales. Although the stories vary, they have something important in common. They are all about a lasting and memorable connection between a human and a cat.

Our book is for everyone who loves and cherishes cats. What sets our book apart is the way these stories have been collected and how they are told. They are told by the teller at the neighborhood bank, by the post office clerk who sells you stamps, by your next-door neighbor, or by your sister-in-law. These stories are not just about a pet cat but are instead about the ways in which people relate to these intriguing companions. Some of these stories are sad, some are heartwarming, and some are hilarious. In their own way, all of them are amazing.

Let the *Cat Tales* begin!

Cat'n Around Catskill 2008

The two Lindas and I were driving up the Taconic State Parkway to Catskill, New York, with excited anticipation. It was September 21, the last day of summer; and as we headed upstate, we could see hints of fall color everywhere, marking the beginning of autumn and the end of a summer that went all too fast. Our goal was to bid on and win one of the painted cats that had been on exhibit on Main Street in Catskill all summer long. It was time to auction off the cats at a gala event at the historic Catskill Point, which sits scenically on the majestic Hudson River. The proceeds from the sale of the cats would then be divided between the artist and local cat shelters in and around the area.

"Drive faster," I complained to Linda, the designated driver.

"Why?" she said. "I'm going the speed limit."

"That's too slow," I replied.

The other Linda, whom we call Lin to avoid confusion, sat in the back. "Settle down, you two," she said. "We left plenty of time to get there, so there is no rush. Sit back and enjoy the ride for Pete's sake."

We'd bought our tickets to the gala event months prior, and I just wanted to be there already. But Lin was right, the scenery was spectacular, so I quieted down and tried to relax.

An hour and a half later, in spite of Linda's painstakingly slow driving, we arrived in the town of Catskill. Thanks to GPS, we didn't get lost and found the building where the gala was to take place. There were people milling about everywhere, wearing all manner of cat adornments. There were cats painted on shirts and hats, and there were lots and lots of cat jewelry. We were no exception. I even wore my Bentley denim jacket for the occasion, a jacket I wear near and dear to my heart and that I consider to have magical and lucky powers.

The excitement continued to build as we approached the entrance to the pavilion. We handed in our tickets and began to meander around the grounds. From the open-walled pavilion, we had a breathtaking view of the Hudson River. The sky was clear, the air crisp. It was a perfect setting and a perfect day for the auction.

After signing up for an auction number (I got number 12, a number I like and consider lucky), I entered the pavilion. The cats were displayed on the right, and I walked over to them. They took my breath away. They were so much more amazing in person than they were in the photographs we had seen online. Music was being piped in through the PA system, and "What's New Pussycat?" by Tom Jones was the first song. There were sixty-two cats sitting on display, and everyone walked around and admired them, deciding which ones they wanted to bid on and bring home. There was *Phil, the Philatelic Cat; A Starry Night in Catskill; Fine Living Feline; Wet Your Whiskers;* just to name a few. One was more beautiful and more creative than the next. We heard oohs and aahs everywhere. Had we stumbled into cat heaven? I began to look for the one I had come to bid on, *Cat Tales.* She was number 29 on the auction block, and I found her sitting right in the middle of the pack. I had only seen her in a photograph and found her colors more vibrant and her design more imaginative than I expected. I had to have her. I worried; did anyone else come for her too?

Where were the two Lindas? I found them buying raffle tickets for the one cat they were raffling off, *Kitty Buffet.* I never win anything but decided to buy a raffle ticket anyway.

The cats on display

"We'll never win," I said.

"I'm going to win this cat," Linda declared defiantly.

"Dream on," I replied.

"I will dream. You'll see," Linda said once again.

After entering the raffle, we went back to look the cats over one last time. Each time we looked at them, we saw something different. The aero cat's eyes lit up like headlights on an airplane, and at the tips of his wings, he had flashing lights. It was hard to stop looking at them, but my stomach began to growl.

"Let's eat," I suggested. They had a wonderful buffet set out, with tortellini, mozzarella and tomatoes, roll-ups, meatballs, scallops wrapped in bacon, cookies, and a large chocolate cake in the shape of one of the cats—*The Kit Kat Cat*. We took our plates outside so that we could enjoy the fresh autumn air and look out on to the spectacular views. We also began to strategize. When should I start bidding, and how high was I willing to go to get her? If I didn't end up winning her, was I willing to bid on another cat, and if so, which one? Our nervous excitement was growing as two o'clock approached, the time set to begin the auction.

We went into the building to find seats, as it was quickly filling up with the three hundred or so people that had come to the event. It was time to get focused. The auctioneer took his position, and the first cat was set out on the auction block.

Mikado on the auction block

The excitement was palpable as the bidding got higher and higher. One thousand, two thousand, three thousand, how high would people go to get their cat? I tentatively bid on number 5, *Sweet Dreams*, because he reminded me of Bentley; but Lin pushed my arm down, telling me to hold out for the one I wanted, the one I came for. I shot my arm up again for *Cat House Cat*, number 21, but stopped short of winning her. They were practice runs. We were getting closer as they brought up numbers 22, 23, 24, 25, 26, 27, and 28; and then finally, there she was on the block—*Cat Tales*. The bidding began at $300. I had come with a limit of what I was willing to spend, $1,500. Some of the others had sold for well over $2,000 and some over $3,000 already. The Lindas were dead silent as the bidding started. At $500, I raised my number 12 in the air. There were several other bidders, and the price quickly rose to $900, then $1,000. Some of the bidders stopped bidding, and it was between me and one other bidder. I went to $1,100, he to $1,200, I to $1,300. Oh my god, would I get her? He went to $1,400; I held my breath and put my number 12 in the air for the last time at $1,500. Going once, going twice, gone!

The two Lindas screamed and hugged me. I sat in disbelief in the middle of these two crazy cat people with the broadest Cheshire cat grin on my face. If I had won a million-dollar lottery, I don't think I could have been happier. Linda had a sore throat from yelling so much, and Lin had a headache from Linda's shouts. I had won the cat I came for; *Cat Tales* was mine.

They continued to auction off the rest of the cats. I could finally relax and enjoy the bidding of others. One of the cats fetched $5,400, and several others went for well over $4,000. It was a very successful auction, and what made it even better was knowing that many shelter cats would now be better off.

It was time to go pay for my cat, which I had to do outside the pavilion. I didn't realize that they were about to announce the winner of the raffle cat, *Kitty Buffet*. I went back inside to collect my cat and look for the Lindas. I couldn't find them anywhere. Suddenly, I heard screaming from the far end of the pavilion. I looked over and saw Linda and Lin standing next to *Kitty Buffet*. I ran over wondering what all the yelling was about.

"I won him," she shouted.

"Get out! You're pulling my leg," I said.

"Yes, I did. I really did. I told you I would win," she said, proudly displaying her new cat.

"Unbelievable."

Linda and *Kitty Buffet*

What a day we had shared together, the two Lindas and I. As much as we hated for the day to end, it was time to go. I was carrying my cat out of the building when a woman ran over to me.

"I'm the artist," she said. "Thank you so much for buying my cat."

"Thank you for creating her," I replied.

Roxanne, the artist, the cat, and I

We strapped *Cat Tales* in the backseat with Lin, and *Kitty Buffet* rode in the back of the SUV, standing up so he could look out the window.

"Slow down," I said to Linda. "You're driving way too fast."

"Humph," she replied.

We stopped at a farm stand on our way home to get pies and apple cider doughnuts. The ride back had such a different feel to it than the ride up, a relaxed excitement. As I enjoyed my doughnut, spilling sugar all over Linda's freshly vacuumed car, I wondered about all the people who were at the auction willing to spend a day and thousands of dollars on these cats. We had all been brought together by these works of cat art, all shared this collective experience, but each in our own particular way. What were their reasons for wanting these cats? What were their stories?

The two Lindas and I at Cat'n Around Catskill 2008

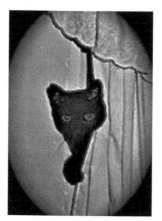

Bastet

Bastet was a mythological sacred cat in ancient Egypt. Her name literally means "devouring lady." She was a renowned and beloved goddess of sunrise, music, dance, pleasure, as well as family, fertility, and birth. Some even believed her to be immortal and more important than humans. Anyone caught harming or killing a cat, even by accident, was punished by death.

Cats played an important part in Egyptian life by keeping the vermin out of the granaries, thereby protecting the food supplies.

All things come to an end, and so did Bubastis, the town where Bastet reigned. Bubastis was destroyed by the Persians (no pun intended) in 350 BC. Today only rubble remains. Among the ruins there is the famous cat cemetery where so many beloved cats journeyed to the other realm.

A Prayer to Bastet

Beloved Bastet, mistress of happiness and bounty, twin of the Sun God, slay the evil that afflicts our minds as you slew the serpent Apep. With your graceful stealth, anticipate the moves of all who perpetrate cruelties and stay their hands against the children of light. Grant us the joy of song and dance and ever watch over us in the lonely places in which we must walk.[*]

You may wish to take a moment to honor this great ancient Egyptian goddess. Light a green candle (Bastet's sacred color) and be nice to a cat, her cherished animal.

---

[*] http://www.moggies.co.uk/bastet/bastet.html

Rena and Heidi

As a veterinarian, I am often asked what the hardest thing I have to do is. Without a doubt, it is putting a beloved pet down. The bond that forms between owner and cat can be so strong and so important that coming to the decision is often next to impossible. It doesn't seem to matter the age of the pet or how long they have been with their owner. We don't want to say good-bye; we don't want to let go even when we know it is the right thing to do. The act of intentionally ending a life, even out of love, is something we all struggle with. Euthanasia is legal and an accepted practice in veterinary medicine, and I have performed this task perhaps hundreds of times. I thought I understood all the emotions that went along with it, until Rena Principi called.

One day, my office received a phone call from an elderly woman who was living in the Gardens, an assisted living facility at Glen Hill in Danbury, Connecticut, with her cat. Many such facilities now allow residents to keep their cats with them because experts have come to realize the many benefits of pet companionship. Rena called to find out if I would come to Glen Hill to take care of her elderly cat. She had some concerns and said she would explain it all upon my arrival. Since I often do house calls, I saw no reason not to take on this new patient. I was impressed with this facility for allowing their residents to keep their pets with them, so I was particularly eager to see the place and to meet Rena and her cat.

We set up an appointment the following week to go out to Glen Hill to meet with Rena. It was a beautiful place, welcoming and full of charm. It had the look of someone's home, not that of an assisted living facility. Just the type of place to allow cats, I thought. When Linda, my assistant, and I arrived at the reception desk and told them who we were and why we were there, the staff practically rolled out a red carpet. It was very clear that everyone was very fond of Rena. We walked by a large living room where some of the residents were watching television, and I asked if Rena was among them. No. We were told she was in her room, with her cat, where she spent most of her time. A notice on the door told everyone to watch out for the cat and not to leave the door open. I couldn't help but smile at the cautionary sign as I pictured her cat running through the corridors, sneaking into other rooms in search of adventure.

Rena's room was cozy and inviting. She welcomed us in and immediately introduced us to Heidi, the love of her life.

"Heidi is eighteen years old and seems to be ailing. She seems to be losing weight and doesn't eat as well as she used to," she told us. "I am dying of cancer, and Heidi is all I have left. I would like you to keep her in good health for me because without her, I have nothing to live for," she said. Rena was being completely honest with me. She continued, "I never married, and I have no children. I have one sister who lives far away who I never see. Can you do this for me, for Heidi? We need each other."

The enormity of what she had just told me was sinking in and left me speechless. I had never met a more forthright person in my life. She wasn't afraid of dying and knew it was going to happen. She had no illusions of a miracle cure, not for her and not for her cat. She had accepted that this was the inevitable end and was at peace with it. Rena was no longer worried about herself, only Heidi.

When I finally took it all in and could speak, I told her I would be honored to make her cat a patient of mine. I then turned my attention to Heidi. She was a black-and-white cat, what is known as a tuxedo cat because it looks like the cat is wearing a tuxedo. Many of the cats I see in their homes are under the bed or behind a sofa when I arrive. They know exactly where to position themselves under things so I cannot reach them from any angle, which has often left me in some rather compromising positions. Not Heidi. She was friendly and approachable. She voluntarily jumped up on the bed and greeted me. I proceeded to examine her, going through my usual routine, starting at the tip of the ears and working my way back. I checked her ears, mouth, eyes, throat, going slowly down the torso until I reach her tail. Then I listened to her heart with my stethoscope and gently palpated her abdomen. I didn't find anything that alarmed me so far. Other than looking a bit thin, she seemed in good shape for her age. I drew some blood to run tests that fully assess her health, checking kidney function, liver function, blood sugar, and so on. Heidi was quite the trooper, allowing me to poke and prod her until I was satisfied I had examined her thoroughly.

After my examination of Heidi, Rena began to tell us about her life. From her dresser drawer, she pulled out her photo album and showed us pictures over tea and cookies. I genuinely liked Rena, enjoying her hospitality and our conversation. When it was time to go, I told Rena I would call her the next day with the blood test results, and we would then discuss how best to keep Heidi healthy and happy. Heidi meowed and trotted off to the perch on the windowsill. When we left, we could see Heidi's beautiful gold eyes looking at us through the slits in the curtains, and it made me smile.

The next day, I got the blood test results, and everything looked good except for Heidi's kidney function. Unfortunately, I see a lot of failing kidneys among cats in their advancing years, and Heidi was no exception. However, I felt that with a change to a lower protein diet and fluid therapy as needed, we could keep Heidi going in comfort for quite some time. I called Rena and gave her the news.

Over the next three months, we visited Rena and Heidi weekly. These visits became special for all of us. Over tea and conversation, we got to know more and more about this wonderful woman. She told us about never finding the right man to marry and her regrets that she never had children. She told us about how much she enjoyed gardening and her passion for cooking. Rena willingly shared her life with us, and although we knew her cancer was painful, she never once showed it. Interwoven into the fabric of the last eighteen years of her life was her constant companion, Heidi. She helped her through the tough times and shared in the good times. She helped her in transition to Glen Hill when the time came that she could no longer take care of herself. At every visit, I checked Heidi, and although she was slowing down, her quality of life still seemed good. Rena and Heidi had a remarkable relationship, and each and every time I went there, I marveled over the depth and breadth of it. Rena doted on Heidi, offering her only the finest cat food. Her shelves were lined with a large variety of cat food because she wanted to be certain Heidi would never get bored with the selection. Heidi was always attentive to Rena, making certain she was nearby, purring within earshot, and giving a lick when needed.

On one of my visits, Rena posed a question to me that I had never been asked before. She told me her cancer was getting worse, and she didn't know how much longer she had. She was worried about Heidi and what would become of her if she were to die before Heidi. She asked me if I would put Heidi to sleep when she herself were to pass. In addition, she wanted to be buried with her cat and could I arrange for that to happen. For the second time since I'd met Rena, I was speechless.

First of all, I didn't know whether it was possible or even legal to do such a thing. Could one be buried with a pet? Secondly, was it ethical to end Heidi's life, perhaps prematurely, so that she could rest with her owner? I told Rena I would look into the matter and get back to her. As it turned out, it was legal for Heidi to be put with Rena. Heidi would have to be cremated, and the urn containing her ashes could then be placed in Rena's casket. I then thought through my next question: was it right to put Heidi to sleep? Rena was concerned that no one would take care of her, given her advanced age and kidney disease. Besides this, she also felt that Heidi would not be able to live without her. I couldn't disagree. No one would take on the responsibility for her care. How much time did Heidi have anyway? Although one can never put an exact time on how long a cat will live with kidney failure, it usually isn't very long, perhaps a couple of months. If Heidi had been younger and in better health, I might have made a different decision, but she wasn't, and I ultimately knew that respecting Rena's wish was the right thing to do. I called Rena to tell her that I would make sure her final request was granted. It gave Rena great relief and comfort to know that we were going to do this for her, and truth be told, I felt both humbled and honored to be entrusted with this task. Heidi and Rena had come this far together, helping each other every step of the way, so it seemed only fitting that their journey continue as one.

I made arrangements with Rena's nurse to let me know when she was near death, as cremation arrangements had to be made, and the timing of this had to be just right. When the nurse finally called, all our hearts sank. We had become so fond of Rena and Heidi and our weekly visits we didn't want to let go. Rena was moved to the hospital, and the staff was taking care of Heidi at Glen Hill. Heidi, we were also told, was not doing well. I told the nurse to have Heidi brought over to the office, and we would do what we needed to do. The time had come for us to live up to our end of the bargain.

We received a call from the hospital that Rena had died. It is even possible that they went at the exact same moment. When I think about Rena and Heidi, I am still astounded by the depth of their relationship and by what they were able to give and do for each other. I am overcome with admiration and feel very lucky to have been a part of their lives, even if briefly. These life-and-death decisions are never ever easy. But I also know that the hardest decisions grant us the opportunity for the most meaning and the most satisfaction in our lives.

In the end, the urn containing Heidi's ashes was placed beside Rena, where it would stay for all eternity. And when I think of that, I smile.

Rena's obituary appeared in the local paper the next day, and here is what it said:

OBITUARIES

Rena Principi

Rena Principi, 84, of Ridgefield, passed away peacefully at Danbury Hospital Dec. 12, 2005, after a long and courageous battle with cancer.

A lifelong resident of Ridgefield, Rena was born May 18, 1921, daughter of Alessandro and Adella (Eppoliti) Principi, immigrants from Italy. Her father was a gardener for the Anne Richardson estate, which is now Richardson Park.

Rena graduated from Ridgefield High School in 1939. She began her career as a secretary at Schlumberger-Doll Research and retired after 27 years.

Rena was a master gardener and an accomplished cook. She loved the town of Ridgefield and always appreciated the friendships of many that were developed over the years.

Heidi, her cat for many years, provided her with good company and companionship.

Grieving a Beloved Cat in Ancient Egypt

Egyptian families kept cats in the house as homage to the gods. A strange and interesting piece of history is that when their cat died, the entire family would shave off their eyebrows as a way of showing their grief. If they did not do this, they might very well become unlucky. The family would remain in mourning until their eyebrows grew back. Sometimes, they had the mummified remains of the cat buried at Bastet's temple necropolis in Bubastis.

So now, if you see a person with their eyebrows gone, give them your sympathies and ask them when their cat died.

The Story of Linda and Mittens

My parents were born and raised in Tagliacozzo, Italy, a small town on the side of a mountain about fifty miles from Rome. To them, animals were meant for food or to help with the farming, not for companionship. They immigrated to this country as teenagers in the early 1950s for a better life. My entire extended family settled in southern Yonkers, New York. My parents married and had two children: my brother and me. We lived in a suburban family neighborhood comprised of hardworking class people, not too far from the Hudson River. My mother was a seamstress in a high-end dress factory owned by my aunt and uncle, and my father worked on the assembly line at the General Motors assembly plant in North Tarrytown (now Sleepy Hollow), New York.

Houses were similar and close together on the street where I grew up. Yards were small but fenced in. As an Italian family, we naturally had a garden filled with tomatoes, basil, peppers, cucumbers, string beans, Swiss chard, and parsley. My father even tried his hand at growing corn and watermelon, without any success. But everything else was amazing. I always say that my dad can make a rock grow, that his whole body is green, not just his thumb.

We had a huge cherry tree that produced buckets of sour cherries and a small aboveground pool that was in constant use in the summer. Our backyard was always occupied, with my father gardening, my mother hanging out the laundry, and me, my brother, and our friends playing. It was a special place, filled with laughter and birthday parties. Sometimes my uncle came by, bringing a bucket full of baby clams that he just caught, and we all would shuck and eat them raw. We had a barbeque that my father had built himself with beautiful yellow bricks that was constantly ablaze with charcoal, the kind you started with lighter fluid, not with a pilot switch. There was also a hand-built storage shed, cement bench, and back steps, all crafted by my father's hands.

Maybe our backyard was extra special because my father's touches were everywhere. Maybe it was special because this was the scene of my birthday parties year after year, where we always had a Carvel ice-cream cake melting in the hot summer sun. Maybe it was special because it was the one place that, even in this working class neighborhood, there were traces of "the old country." Maybe it was a combination of all these things. However, it was the one house on the block that did not have a cat, and to me that was everything.

I had always adored cats and begged my parents to let me have one. I had books with cats, pictures of cats, clothes with cats on them. My room was filled with kitty stuffed animals and figurines.

My family would call me "cat crazy," and being that I was the only one in my very big Italian family with green eyes, they all said that I had "cat eyes." I always wore that badge with pride. If it involved a cat, I wanted to immerse myself in it.

When I was five, my class went on a field trip to Old McDonald's Farm in Connecticut; my mother came along as chaperone. We walked through all the animal exhibits. There were birds, reptiles, and, to my delight, a cottage filled with cats and newborn kittens. I was in my glory. My group had to move on. They went to the other exhibits and, after a time, realized that I was missing. My mother was frantic until she calmed down long enough to remember about the cat cottage. Of course, that's where they found me.

By this time, it was obvious that my love of cats was more than just a passing fancy. But I was still part of an immigrant Italian family that believed animals didn't belong inside the house.

One day, to my sheer joy, a beautiful, friendly, speckled brown cat walked into our backyard and came toward me, rubbing and purring. He had big green eyes, just like mine. I named him Mittens. In retrospect, I should have called him Kismet. But I already had the name picked out long before he ever showed up in our yard. I had just decided that when I got my own cat, that is what his name would be.

"Can I keep him?" I cried to my mother.

"No, not in the house. Animals belong outside," she replied, just as I'd expected.

Luckily, Mittens was just as determined as I was to make our yard his home. He made the backyard even more of a special place for me because now it was Mittens's domain, his territory. Between Boots, the nasty Siamese cat that would yowl all night to the left of us, and Chibuk and Princess, aloof and proper in their own enchanted flower garden on the right side of our house, here was my beautiful Mittens. Sweet and complacent, he was already a part of me.

"Once you feed a stray cat," my mother would say to me, "he always comes back."

I might have been only eight years old, but my mama didn't raise no fool! I snuck food out to him every day. Sure enough, my mother was right; Mittens kept coming back. I was hoping with time, my parents would accept him as a member of the family.

Mittens was my best friend. Every day, I hurried home from school to be with him. He would sit with me and purr as I did my homework. He would stay in the yard near me while I played with my friends. He was my constant companion; I hated to leave the house and yard because it meant leaving Mittens behind.

Little by little, I began sneaking Mittens into the house. My parents started to get used to seeing him in my arms, and my mother's grocery cart suddenly contained cat food. One morning, I woke up to find Mittens sleeping in a specially made bed just for him in our warm, huge, and sunny kitchen. It made me particularly happy because I knew that it was my mother who had sewn the bed for him.

Although I didn't know it at the time, having Mittens indoors was bothering my parents. After all, none of my cousins had pets. To my extended family, it was considered "disgusting" to have a cat in the house.

One day after school, I went out to the backyard, and I couldn't find Mittens. I walked up and down the street calling his name. I asked all my neighbors, but no one had seen him. He was nowhere to be found, either in the yard or around the neighborhood. When I asked my parents if they had seen Mittens, they told me that he must have run away.

I was inconsolable. I tried to do all the normal things an eight-year-old does. I went to school, played with my friends, and did homework. But things just weren't the same without my Mittens. I was miserable, and I couldn't stop thinking about him. My days and nights, which had been so joyous, were suddenly filled with tears. Where was he? Why would Mittens leave me? I thought he'd loved me as much as I'd loved him.

This went on for two very long weeks. During that time, not a minute went by that I did not think of him. Since my parents told me that Mittens had probably run away, I tried everything to get him to come back to me. I put out his favorite food. I even placed the bed my mother had made for him in the yard in the hope that he would come back.

Just when I thought I would never see Mittens again, I went to the backyard, and to my delight, there he was. My Mittens! He was much thinner than he'd been, but he was back. My parents were shocked too, although they seemed more surprised than happy to see Mittens.

While I was thrilled that Mittens was back, I could see that he was very sick. He had lost weight, his fur was no longer shiny, and he didn't seem to want to play or eat. One night, soon after he'd come home, I was watching TV, and Mittens was next to me. We always shared a huge floor pillow in the living room. The way he was positioned that evening, in retrospect, was quite eerie. He was propped up on his stomach, but he held his paws together almost as if he were praying. I will never forget how he looked that night.

Mittens died the next day.

Many years later, my parents confessed that my father had put Mittens in the trunk of the car and driven him to the General Motors plant in North Tarrytown (the town has since been renamed Sleepy Hollow). My father had seen many unwanted animals "dumped" at GM in his years there; it was something people did at the time. But Mittens had found his way back to me. North Tarrytown was many miles away from our home. How he found his way back is still a complete mystery.

When my mom and dad think back to that time, they can't believe that they actually conspired to get rid of Mittens. In later years, the answer to my question "Can I have a cat?" wasn't always no. When Rocky, a beautiful black-and-white tuxedo cat, came along, my mother welcomed him; in fact, she actually cooked for him. Rocky was the fattest and happiest cat in the neighborhood.

In my eight-year-old mind, I felt it was terribly unfair that Mittens had gone through so much hardship and had come home only to die. But as the years went by, I came to realize that he came back to *me*. I *was* special to him. He must have known that he was dying, and he needed to be with me in his final moments.

Mittens was dumped miles from home. He was sick, and he was dying. Yet, against all odds, he found his way home to me. When I think of him in that prayerful pose, I know that he was looking toward heaven. There is a saying, "Heaven is the place where all the cats you've ever loved are waiting for you." I know that Mittens is waiting there for me. I know that he'll be greeting me at the gates with a bump, a purr . . . and those big green eyes.

The Cat and Its Homing Device

As implausible as it may seem, cats do have a homing ability. There are many documented cases of cats that have found their way home from far distances. There was Ninja, who returned from Washington State to his former residence in Utah, which was 850 miles away. *The Incredible Journey*, a beloved children's movie, depicts both dogs and cats finding their way back home. Although the movie was fiction, it could very well have happened in real life. The homing ability is found in many species of animals, and the cat is no exception. Scientists believe that the cat uses its biological clock, the angle of the sun, and the Earth's magnetic field.

Peter and Henry and Ralph

This is the story of Peter, Henry, and Ralph. Peter is the human, and Henry and Ralph are his cats. Maybe it's the other way around. Maybe Peter is their human, I'm not sure. Henry and Ralph are not ordinary cats. They are Cornish Rexes, a breed affectionately known as Cornies. A Cornish Rex has almost no fur, and what little it does have is short and wavy. Cornies are the finest boned of all the breeds. Because of their lack of fur and bony physique, they are always looking for sources of warmth and are often referred to by their owners as "heat-seeking missiles."

Peter is no ordinary person. He is a modern-day renaissance man. He has created a world-class garden; he is an architect, designer, and much more. He's smart and sassy and really, really funny. It's been an honor to be his friend and veterinarian to his cats for the last fifteen years.

In 1999, Peter lost his sixteen-year-old cat, Burt, to cancer. At about the same time, his other cat, Rosemary, was brutally attacked and killed by a coyote. There are those who cannot be without a cat, and Peter is one of those people. Since I am a compulsive cat-human matchmaker, he asked me to find him a cat. As it happened, I knew someone who had recently adopted a Cornish Rex kitten only to discover that her husband was severely allergic to cats. He was only four months old, a handsome cream-and-white boy. I told Peter I had found the perfect kitten for him and that I would bring it over the following day.

A Cornie can be quite the sight. Skinny, bony, almost without fur, and with huge ears, to the uninitiated eye, they look more like a cross between a rat and a Chihuahua than a cat. But because I live with two of them, Paco and Rosie, and have been bewitched by their beguiling ways, I have come to see them as exquisitely beautiful.

When I opened the crate, the kitten scampered out, all legs and ears.

Peter's first words were, "Ugh, he is so ugly! I don't know if I can live with such an ugly creature. Is he even really a cat?"

My reply was simple. "Peter, keep him here over the weekend, and I'll call you on Monday. If you decide you don't want him, I will come and take him back." I knew something Peter did not know: by Monday, he would be so smitten with this kitten that wild horses could not separate them.

On Monday morning, I called Peter. "Well, do you want me to come and get the kitten?"

"What, are you crazy?" he replied. "He is the most beautiful creature, the most wonderful kitten I have ever seen. No, you cannot have him back!"

Kitten lesson number 1: Beauty is in the eye of the beholder.

Peter named him Henry. Henry happily filled the void left by the sudden loss of both his cats. Laughter over his antics became a daily occurrence. Several months later, I had an opportunity to breed Rosie, and since Henry still had his family jewels, I asked Peter if he thought Henry would like to be a father. He told me to wait a sec; he would ask Henry.

He muffled the phone, but I could hear him shouting, "Henry, do you want to have sex with Rosie? Do you want to make babies?" Peter was always the jokester, always quick with his verbal repartee. "Okay, Henry said yes."

Traditionally, the female is brought to the male for breeding, and so I drove Rosie over to Henry. Three days later, Peter called to ask me what Rosie looked like; he hadn't seen her since shortly after

I dropped her off. I drove back and found Rosie hiding in the far corners of Peter's garage, absolutely terrified. We would have to devise another plan.

I brought Rosie and Henry back with me and put them in the "honeymoon suite." Sixty-five days later, Rosie gave birth to three sweet little kittens, two girls and a blue-and-white boy. Peter missed the birth but came by the very next day to meet his grandchildren.

One by one, he picked them up, saving the boy for last. They were so tiny that they fit in the palm of one hand. It took but a second and Peter was in love with the little blue-and-white boy. "He is mine," he said, and just like that, Peter now had two Cornies.

Kitten lesson number 2: Two Cornies are better than one.

Every week, Peter came to see the babies, took pictures of their growth, and proudly showed them to everyone. Week by week, as we watched the babies grow, our relationship grew from a professional one to a friendship. All of us—Peter, Henry, Rosie, the new babies, and I—were now bonded forever.

The weeks went by quickly for me, slowly for Peter. He would have to wait eight weeks before he could bring his new kitten home. I had them with me every day from the day they were born. Rosie, not wanting to miss sleeping under the covers with me, would carry the kittens on to my bed. She would grip them by their scruffs, carry them across the room, jump on to the bed, and drop them. She was already training them to be under-the-cover kitties.

Finally, at eight weeks of age, the kittens were old enough to leave the nest. The blue-and-white kitten went to live with Peter and Henry. Peter named him Ralph. Peter and Henry and Ralph were perfect together. At night, Henry and Ralph would sleep under the covers with Peter, one on his left side, one on his right side, flanking him, keeping themselves and Peter warm through the night. They were a perfectly balanced family.

Kitten lesson number 3: Families come in all shapes and sizes.

Henry and I share a birthday, and every year, Peter would call to wish me a happy birthday and to thank me for bringing Henry and then Ralph into his life. I, in turn, would sing happy birthday to Henry over the phone, and we would all laugh heartily. That was until November 30, 2007. Peter didn't call me. The day passed, and I didn't hear from him. Was it possible that he forgot? I had a bad feeling, but I let it go as I had dinner plans to go out and have a birthday celebration with my husband. It was 6:00 p.m., and I was alone in the house, waiting for my husband to come home. The phone rang. It was a mutual friend of Peter's and mine. Peter had had a major stroke and was in critical condition. I was in shock. He was only fifty-nine years old and the picture of health. How could this happen? His friend Rob had come by in the morning and found him still in bed, disoriented, barely able to speak or walk. He called for an ambulance and quickly got him to the hospital. Rob later told me that as they were wheeling him into the emergency room, he uttered two words, "the boys." Rob knew immediately what he meant and assured him that he would take care of Ralph and Henry.

Over the next couple of weeks, Peter lay in the hospital. Friends and family came to be by his side night and day. I received daily reports of his status and prayed every day that he would be all right. The world went out of kilter those days and weeks for all of us, but for no one more than Henry and Ralph.

Peter survived the stroke. He was left with major deficits. The right side of his body was severely impaired, and he had almost no use of his right arm and leg. To make matters worse, he could not speak. Peter, the jokester, the most wonderful communicator, could not make words. After he left the hospital, he entered a rehab facility where he lived for several months. Pictures of Ralph and Henry plastered the walls, along with pictures of his beloved garden and home. Always the giver, now it was time for him to take. Love and support came from everywhere. Since he was not able to walk up and down stairs, his friends built an extension in his home so that he could reside on one level. People went every day to tend to

Peter's world-class garden and to make sure Henry and Ralph were OK. More than anything, Peter wanted to get home to Ralph and Henry. They needed him, and he needed them.

Peter finally made it home after several long and hard months of rehab. He can walk and get up and down the stairs now. Ralph and Henry are back to sleeping with him, one on his right and one on his left. I go there every three weeks or so to clean Ralph and Henry's ears and clip their nails, and I have a chance to visit with my friend, Peter.

Peter still can't make many words. He has learned to communicate with vocal sounds more than words—with a facial expression, with a twist of his mouth, or with his one good hand. He uses body language more than words to communicate and let people know what is on his mind, what he is thinking or needing. In this way, he has become much more like our feline companions, who let us know without words what they want and what they feel. In my veterinary practice, I have learned to look closely at my patients because they cannot tell me where it hurts or what happened to them. They often tell me more without words than their owners do with a full vocabulary.

Kitten lesson number 4: You don't need words to communicate; you only need to look closely and pay attention.

It has been a year and a half since Peter's stroke. He is making progress with his walking and his speech, but it is slow and hard for him. Sometimes he gets discouraged and annoyed. Sometimes the people around him get frustrated because they cannot understand what he is trying to communicate. It isn't easy getting used to a new way of living, of making progress at what feels like a snail's pace. When I visit Peter, I find myself missing the Peter that could make the quip, and I feel sad for him.

But then Ralph and Henry will enter the room, give Peter a look that probably says, "The vet is here again? I have to sit and get my ears cleaned again?" They run when they see me pull out the Q-tips, and Peter laughs that hearty laugh I love so much. Ralph and Henry know just how to make Peter smile, without a single word. They don't see the things Peter cannot do. They don't care that he walks with a limp or that words do not come easily to him and that he cannot tell a joke the way he used to. After all, they never got his jokes anyway. And most important, they have their heating pad back.

Peter and Henry and Ralph

Cheshire Cat

This cat's grin is reminiscent of the vagaries of human character or of a prankster. Lewis Carroll's *Alice in Wonderland* brought this smiling cat to life. In the book, Alice first encounters the cat in her house in the kitchen. She later sees him again outside on the branches of a tree where he appears and disappears at will. At one point, the cat disappears slowly, leaving behind his grin, at which point Alice remarks that she has "often seen a cat without a grin but never a grin without a cat." The Cheshire cat has become enmeshed in popular culture. He appears in media, in political cartoons, in movies, television, just to name a few. The British Shorthair cat was the model for the Cheshire cat due to its "smile."

Even if you have never heard of *Alice in Wonderland*, you probably know what is meant by the Cheshire cat's grin. But who knows? Is he the one who ate the canary?

Greg and TiVo

He started out like the rest of them, beautiful, furry, and incredibly adorable. One of five perfect kittens, he was the only orange kitty in the bunch. Aside from his color, it wasn't immediately apparent that he was different. As the litter grew and their personalities began to emerge, it was clear that he wasn't like the others. He was shy, didn't care much to be with his siblings, and avoided all human contact.

He was purchased as a small kitten and was returned just when I started working at the Complete Cat. As a result of a broken relationship, he came back to the clinic when he was fourteen months old. There was something about him that fascinated me, and in hindsight, that "something" is very clear. We temporarily put him in a kitty condo where he would protest all day. I would go to him and talk to him, and his pleas to me were "Meow, meow, meow" or "Get me out of here, but don't look at me, and don't touch me."

My youngest son, Greg, was born a perfect healthy baby. Maybe because he was born at nine pounds thirteen ounces (which I felt every ounce of), he didn't have that wrinkly, cone-shaped newborn look. His alert big blue eyes made him even more engaging. He was always so happy, smiling and cooing all the time. He was the perfect baby.

Greg's voice was all but silenced when he was two years old. My once happy baby stopped making eye contact, stopped talking entirely, and shunned all attempts at affection. He didn't laugh anymore and retreated into his own world. Although I realized that there was something wrong with my child, I had no idea what it could be. Some family members were in denial and saw nothing wrong; others thought it was just a phase that he would grow out of. I took him to see a variety of doctors, but it wasn't until I took him to an audiologist that the word "autism" came up.

Now that we had a diagnosis, we began our path to finding a way back to him. There was speech and occupational therapy, special diets, medication, and megadoses of vitamins. We toyed with chelating, group therapy, and psychiatrist visits. We fought to keep him mainstreamed because we wanted him to learn to be a regular kid. Even a simple activity like going to McDonald's was difficult because Greg could not tell me what he liked and what he didn't like. I would end up purchasing three different kids meals so Greg could have what he wanted. I didn't even know what his favorite color was. I remember saying to one of the many professionals that we sought out to help Greg, "I just want to know my own son."

Obsessions plagued him as well. Shopping became a nightmare because if we passed an aisle with ceiling fans, my once placid baby would scream until I took him to the fans to watch them spin. He could watch them for hours. Heating vents and roads engrossed him. His intricate pencil-drawn maps and cities were detailed right down to the last streetlight. Because of this fascination with roads, we had a ritual every afternoon: going for a ride on the highway. These rides together were more than fine with me because for that half hour ride in the car, I was a part of the world that he would let no one into.

After one of our afternoon road trips, I suggested to Greg that we stop and visit the orange kitty that was returned to us. For two weeks, this visit became part of our daily routine. The parallels between Greg and this cat became crystal clear to me. In the past, we tried to stimulate Greg's personality and social skills by the purchase of lizards, turtles, fish, and even a bunny. I would have brought just about any type of creature into the house if I thought it would have helped our son.

On one of our visits, this shy orange cat that wouldn't make contact with anybody bumped up against Greg. Greg responded by reaching down to pet him on his head, and I saw a long-awaited smile cross his face. They were getting through to each other. Although this may look like a small act to someone else, I knew it was monumental. I knew I was going to be put in the doghouse by my husband for this, but I found a carrier and took him home.

Now he needed a name. Since times had changed since we named our last cat, Betamax, we named the new kitty TiVo. He wasn't an easy cat to warm up to. If we petted him or gave him any sort of affection, he would protest loudly. He hated being picked up. I had never seen a cat like this before. He wasn't mean or nasty. He never hissed or scratched. He was just very much in his own world.

As the weeks went by, I would catch my husband, John, talking to TiVo. I would see my son, Johnny, trying to play with him, but it was Greg who was forming the strongest bond. There was TiVo bumping only Greg and sleeping on his bed. He had warmed up to us, but it was from Greg that he would welcome affection, and it was Greg that was actually *giving* the affection, not something that came easily to either one of them. Greg had formed a bond with another living being. They were getting closer and closer and were teaching each other the value of friendship.

I have been told that with autistic children, there is a time when you actually grieve the child that you thought was born to you. There are five stages of grief—denial, anger, bargaining, depression, acceptance—and our family was going through all these stages. The unconditional acceptance between TiVo and Greg was a life lesson for all of us. If a cat could accept Greg for who he was and see what was inside of him, why couldn't we? TiVo helped us accept that Greg didn't need to be "fixed." He was perfect just the way he was.

The shy redheaded cat and the boy that no one knew have brought out the best in each other. Greg and TiVo continue to grow. They both still struggle with social interactions, but they are both more articulate (TiVo meows more than ever) and are both more affectionate. Greg has learned from TiVo that it's not so bad to be who you are even if you are a little different, and TiVo has learned from Greg that people aren't so scary.

However, Greg and TiVo are not the only ones that have grown from this very special relationship. Perhaps I've learned most of all. I have become a more patient person. I am not as afraid of the future, and my faith has been strengthened. Who would have thought that a cat could have brought so much into all our lives?

Greg and TiVo

TiVo on the bed

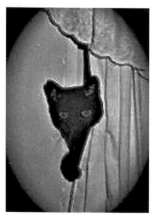

Presidential Cats

It is probably safe to say that Socks Clinton is the most famous first cat. There have been so many first dogs, which begs the question, which were our feline-loving presidents?

The first official first cat was Abraham Lincoln's cat, Tabby. Not many kitties followed, but after Tabby, here is the official White House first cat list:

* George W. Bush — India (also known as Willie)
* Bill Clinton — Socks
* Jimmy Carter — Misty Malarky Ying Yang
* Gerald Ford — Shan
* John F. Kennedy — Tom Kitten
* Calvin Coolidge — Tiger, Smoky (a bobcat), and two lion cubs
* Woodrow Wilson — Puffins
* Theodore Roosevelt — Tom Quartz and Slippers
* William McKinley — Valeriano Weyler and Enrique DeLome
* Rutherford Hayes — Piccolomini and Miss Pussy

And then there was Martin Van Buren who felt that he needed something a bit more exotic. A gift from the sultan of Oman, the White House was the home to the first tiger cubs. (Hate to be the one to clean that litter box!)

A Tale of Two Sexes

Sometimes things are not how they appear. Take for example the sex of a cat. As newborns, it can be very hard to tell if they are male or female. Many times, I have had clients come in with their new kittens, only to inform them that they were not the sex they thought they were. Princess quickly becomes Prince, George becomes Georgia, and Beatrice becomes Bruno. Sometimes Dave just remains Dave even though he is a she. Marilyn remains Marilyn although she is a he. It can get very confusing. Sometimes this confusion of the sexes can become even more complicated.

Nancy, a breeder of Scottish Folds and a regular at the office, brought her new calico kitten, Suzy, in for her first checkup. She had intentions to use her in her breeding program when she became old enough. Since virtually all calicos are female, I had no reason to question the sex of this kitten. In the extremely rare instance that a calico is a male, he is sterile, but I had never seen one of these cats and thought I never would. They are one in a million. Suzy's checkup went well; she was a perfectly healthy specimen. I gave her a clean bill of health, and with the good news that all was normal, Nancy took her home. Several months later, when the kitten turned seven months old, Nancy called the office.

"Tell Dr. Eisen that Suzy is a boy. She has two round protuberances under her tail. They just seemed to appear out of nowhere," she told the receptionist.

My first reaction was that Nancy was imagining things. I had seen this kitten only a few short months before, and I was certain she was a female. My second reaction was, I just had to see this. I told my receptionist to call Nancy right back and have her bring Suzy in immediately. Was it possible I would see my first male calico? For

Nancy, this was not what she had hoped for as she had intended to breed this cat, but for me, it was an opportunity to see an anomaly that I thought I would never witness in my career. I honestly thought Nancy was making this all up, seeing things that weren't there. In the past, Nancy had been prone to exaggeration. Still, I took my camera out just in case. This was an event worth photographing.

Nancy came right over, and we ushered her and Suzy to the exam room. The entire staff was there to see if the "protuberances" were actually real. Linda held the camera as I picked up Suzy's tail. By George, there they were. Two full-size testicles were staring at me. Or so I thought.

"Well, Nancy, it seems you were right this time. These certainly look like testicles to me," I said, trying to contain my excitement.

"What do I do now?" she asked.

"I'm afraid we'll have to neuter her or him."

We scheduled the surgery for the following day. I couldn't wait to tell all my associates that I had seen a male calico. After I removed the protuberances and examined them, however, they didn't look like typical testicles. They had a slightly odd shape to them, looking more like ovaries than testicles. Were they testicles or ovaries? And if they were ovaries, what were they doing way down there? This was getting odder by the second. There was only one way to find out. I examined them under the microscope. If they were testicles, I should see sperm; if they were ovaries, I should see eggs. Everyone was hovering around the microscope.

"Well," the staff asked me in unison, "what is it?"

"I see eggs, hundreds and hundreds of them."

It turned out that Suzy was a female after all. Not the male calico I had hoped for, but a very interesting case nevertheless, and a case I would probably never see again. The only remaining question was how this cat's ovaries ended up where testicles normally are.

My only explanation was this: initially, the ovaries and testicles start out in the same place—in the abdomen, behind the kidneys. During development, if the cat is male, the hormone testosterone causes the testicles to descend and take a route that travels down through the abdomen, through what is called the inguinal ring, finally ending up on the outside of the abdomen underneath the tail. If the cat is female, the hormone estrogen will keep the ovaries where they belong, remaining behind the kidneys. Suzy must have produced too much testosterone, sending the ovaries on the route the testicles take, but she did not have enough testosterone to make her a male. Confusing?

"So, is Suzy a boy or a girl?" Nancy wanted to know when she came to pick her up.

"I guess she's a girl," I replied. It was the best answer I could give her.

I hoped that Nancy wouldn't discard this cat as worthless now that she couldn't be bred. So often, these cats end up in shelters or, even worse, destroyed. I had seen this all too often. When they left the office, I reminded Nancy just how special her kitty was.

I thought I would never see anything like this again. I had almost forgotten about Suzy when Jen Frey called. Jen had decided she wanted to try her hand at breeding British Shorthairs and had purchased a beautiful lilac-and-white female kitten. Jen was particularly excited because at her first cat show, the judges were all very impressed with her kitten. She was so big and robust that she looked like a boy, they all remarked. Jen had high hopes of showing her to grand champion and then breeding this fabulous specimen. She named her Elena.

When Elena turned seven months old, the office received a phone call from Jen.

"Something is wrong with Elena," Jen said. "She isn't going into heat, and her urine is smelling really strong, like a male. And she has these swellings under her tail. They look really weird."

Elena wasn't a calico, but still, she had been a girl. I was certain of that. Could this be happening again? It would be like lightning striking in the same place twice.

The next day, Jen was at the office with Elena. I pulled up Elena's tail, and once again, I saw protuberances on a cat that was in theory a female. But this time was different. The swellings looked completely abnormal. It looked like Elena had both male and female external sex organs, both a vagina and a penis. Could Elena be a true hermaphrodite? Could she be both male and female? I knew this would be a huge disappointment for Jen, a potential breeder, but another enormously interesting case for me.

"Now what?" Jen asked.

"I'm afraid I'll have to neuter her or him." Amazed that I was saying these words for a second time.

I removed the so-called testicles and examined them under the microscope. This time, I saw neither sperm nor eggs. What did this mean? Again I questioned, is Elena a boy or a girl?

I told Jen that I thought Elena was a hermaphrodite, with more male characteristics than female. It was the best answer I could give. Elena has kept her name, and in Jen's eyes, she will always be a girl; but of course, she will never have kittens.

I worry that when cats don't meet breeders' expectations, they will be tossed aside or loved and cared for less. But in these two most unusual cases, they are loved even more. Nancy and Jen always have a good story to tell about these "girls." After all, they are both one in a million.

Elena

Suzy

Songs About Cats

There have been many unforgettable songs by popular artists written about cats as well. Some have done very well in all genres of music and climbed various music charts in the Billboard 100. Some of these songs include the following:

"Honky Cat" by Elton John

"Stray Cat Strut" by the Stray Cats

"What's New Pussycat?" by Tom Jones

"Cool For Cats" by Squeeze

"Year of the Cat" by Al Stewart

"The Cat's in the Cradle" by Harry Chapin

"Cat Scratch Fever" by Ted Nugent

There are also songs about big cats:

What *Rocky* fan doesn't remember "Eye of the Tiger" by Survivor?

Or "The Lion Sleeps Tonight" by the Tokens? ("Aweemba way aweemba way." Come on, I know you're singing this one now!)

The list goes on and on, but we saved the best to close out this list. Let's not forget Disney's "Everybody Wants to be a Cat"!

Suzanne and the Valley of the Dolls

When I first opened the Complete Cat Clinic in 1991, I had a neighbor that was a dialysis nurse at the local hospital. Since we were both involved in health care, we would often sit out on our front lawns when weather permitted and talk shop. One day, she mentioned that she had a patient that was "really" into cats. Her name was Suzanne, and she had the unfortunate distinction of being the longest-standing dialysis patient at the hospital. She was only thirty-two years old and had been on dialysis for sixteen years. I did the math and realized that this poor woman had spent half her life undergoing dialysis. My neighbor continued to tell me that Suzanne had a lot of cats, although she wasn't sure exactly how many. She also knew that Suzanne would love to talk to me and asked if it would be all right if she gave her my phone number. I told her it would be more than all right and to please have her call me anytime she liked. We talked a little more of other things—cats and kidney failure, how dialysis is not an option for cats, and the future of kidney transplants. With the sun going down, we finally said our good-nights and retreated to our homes.

Several weeks later, I heard from Suzanne. She called the clinic and asked if I would take her on as a new client. Since I offered house calls, she also asked if I would be willing to come to her house to meet her and her cats. She mentioned that she had a lot of cats, too many to bring in the office. An appointment was scheduled for the following week.

I offered house calls for a variety of reasons—for cats that don't travel well, for people that cannot travel, and for multiple-cat households. It is a well-needed and appreciated service. Sometimes seeing the environment in which the cat lives can even help in making a diagnosis.

As I prepared my house call bag for my visit with Suzanne, I wondered what her house would be like, what she would be like. I knew she was a very sick young woman who had a lot of cats. Would the house be dirty? Would it smell? Would the cats be well taken care of? Would Suzanne talk to me about her life? What would I say in response?

I drove up her driveway and was immediately impressed with her neatly manicured yard. She saw me coming and greeted me at the door, letting me know I had arrived at the right place. She was a well-dressed petite woman with big brown eyes and soft blond hair. Although she was only thirty-two years old, she walked with a cane. I could see that she had been through unimaginable health problems in her very short life, but she was so gracious and welcoming that my nervousness began to evaporate. She had that "don't feel sorry for me" attitude.

It was a small house, all on one floor. She told me there were eighteen cats and that she was a breeder of Ragdolls. A Ragdoll, named for its tendency to go floppy when picked up, is a big lovable cat with silky fur. The coat is a combination of dark points, light body color, and beautiful China blue eyes. She named her cattery Valley of the Dolls after her last name, Vallee. How clever, I thought. When I entered the house, I saw cats everywhere. Some were in the living room, lounging in the rays of sun coming through the bay window. She had a bedroom set up for nursing mothers and their babies. In her bedroom, she had the playful toddlers running and jumping around everywhere. The entire house was set up and organized around the cats and their needs. We went from room to room as she introduced me to all her exquisite cats, and I proceeded to examine them one by one. They were impeccably clean, as was the house itself. Her cats were some of the most beautiful and well taken care of felines I had ever seen. Some were top show cats, she bragged, and I could see why.

After examining all the cats, we sat for a cup of tea and conversation. She opened up and told me about her life. A chemical at the plant where she worked sixteen years ago had destroyed her kidney function. It was a devastating event that left her essentially crippled for the rest of her life. She was engaged to a wonderful man at the time, and they married the following year. He was still by her side and a tremendous support for her. But it was the cats that really kept her going. They lifted her spirits and gave her something to live for on a daily basis. Even in her darkest hours, if she thought about her cats, she could get through anything. I could see the proof of that as I looked around the kitchen where we sat. Every cat in the room looked at her adoringly, and it was obvious that the cats loved her every bit as much as she loved them.

After my first house call at the Valley of the Dolls, as I came to call the house, I would hear from Suzanne from time to time when she had concerns about one thing or another—a pregnant cat, a fading kitten, a spraying tom. We developed a great relationship, and we grew to respect and like one another very much.

One day, sitting out on the front porch with my neighbor, she told me that Suzanne was not doing well. She had been on dialysis for so long that they could no longer find a healthy vein in which to insert an IV. She would be starting peritoneal dialysis. This type of dialysis does have its advantages: it can be done at home and can be done while sleeping. Suzanne was able to see the bright side of almost everything, and she saw the upside of this too. Those hours that she normally sat in the hospital, she could now spend at home with her cats. My neighbor also confided in me that Suzanne would love the opportunity to work at the clinic, in any capacity. She wanted to learn as much as she could about cats and their care. Yes, she was sick and often didn't feel well, but even a few hours a week would be enough.

I offered Suzanne a receptionist position for six hours a week. She would cover the Thursday evening hours and the busy Saturday mornings. I only offered her six hours a week at an hourly rate, but Suzanne felt like she had just won the lottery. She showed up, ready to work, no matter how tough things were for her. I knew she was beginning her home dialysis, and her life was far from easy, what with all the adjustments that had to be made, but she never showed it. She was always ready for work and always had an infectious smile on her face.

She only worked there for two months when I received a call from her husband. Suzanne had developed an infection in her abdomen from the dialysis and couldn't come to work. She had been admitted to the hospital in critical condition, and he didn't know what the future held or if there would be a future for Suzanne. Before she entered the hospital, she made him promise not to neglect the cats, which he swore to do. I assured him that if he needed me in any capacity, I would be there.

Suzanne never made it back home. She died a week later from the infection. Her husband called to tell me of her passing and to let me know when and where her funeral would take place. Suzanne and I only knew each other for a very brief time, but I felt we made an important and meaningful connection. Sadly, I went to her funeral to pay my respects and to honor this woman who lovingly created the most splendid Ragdoll cats I had ever seen. When I entered the funeral parlor, the first thing I saw was the floral arrangement over her casket. It was extraordinarily beautiful, and it was in the shape of a cat. It was deeply moving, and it was perfect.

Suzanne will never be forgotten, not just by her family and friends, but also by the entire cat fancy. Her legacy will live on forever through the Valley of the Dolls Ragdolls that she so carefully and tenderly brought to this world.

A Ragdoll cat

Suzanne Vallee at the front desk

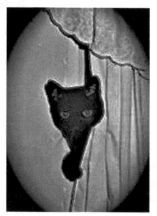

The First Cat Shows

The first official cat show took place at the Crystal Palace in London on July 16, 1871. Harrison Weir, a writer, artist, and cat lover extraordinaire, organized it. Using his artistic skills, Weir had drawn a poster to advertise this show, depicting a black cat's head on yellow paper. Cats came from far and wide. It was a resounding success, and shows were held there every year until December 1936, when sadly, it was destroyed by fire on the eve of the National Cat Show.

However, cat lovers were hooked and found other venues to display their beloved cats. They continued to hold cat shows in and around the London area.

Ten years later, the first cat show was held in America. As reported by the *New York Times* on Sunday, March 6, 1881:

> Manager Bunnel stood in the center of his museum on Broadway, his hands in his hair, utterly perplexed, late last night. He was surrounded by cats in cages, cats in wooden boxes, cats in hand boxes, cats in bags, half of them yelling, spitting, and scratching, as mad as cats can be in uncomfortable quarters and in a strange place. A deep scratch on his nose and three fingers tied up in oil and rags told how inexperienced he was in the way of cats. As fast as the cages were completed and the cats were placed in little sections, each one alone, they settled down for the night, and silence reigned.

What a show!

In 2009, cat shows are held internationally, drawing thousands of spectators all across the cat-loving globe.

Patrick and Cubby

On most mornings, you will find Patrick and his cat companion, Cubby, across the street from Pike Place Market in Seattle, Washington. He comes with his setup, an open booth with a flat surface where Cubby calmly sits. Cubby, without having to do anything, commands your attention. Patrick, a colorful man with an easy rapport, does the talking; Cubby, a charismatic presence, draws you in. They are not there to entertain, although they are very entertaining, but to ask for donations to help with the costs of the unwanted cats that Patrick takes into his home. They are also there to educate the public about homelessness in cats and about the true nature of the feline, something Patrick is an expert on. His goal is to socialize these unwanted cats using his cat communication techniques, make them feel wanted, and place them in loving homes.

Pike Place Market is a hubbub of activity. Tourists from all over the world come here to experience the unique atmosphere of the market. Locals come to do their shopping or have a bite to eat at one of the many restaurants. Fish are flying, musicians are playing, and crafters are selling their wares. At any given time, there are hundreds of people walking through and around the market. None of this fazes Cubby, who sits on his perch like a Buddha.

Remarkable as this is, what is even more remarkable is the relationship between Patrick and Cubby. It is clear that these two have something very special between them. How did this all begin? In past visits to Seattle, I never had the courage to approach them. I always wanted to, but instead I would just watch them along with the rest of the crowd, always donating something before I left. Ask a question, make a friend, I thought; and with that in mind, I found the courage to go up and introduce myself. I told him I was a fellow cat lover and cat veterinarian. It turned out all I had to do was ask. Patrick was more than happy to share his love story:

> I'll tell you about how I acquired Cubby. We don't have any "puppy mill" pet stores in Seattle anymore, but six years ago, there were still a couple; one had over two hundred complaints. We went there to buy all four cats. They had to give them to little old ladies who would spoil them. (We never sell cats). Cubby was one of these, about four months old. The first time I saw Cubby, there was urine dripping onto his head from the cage above him, and there was kitty litter clay caked between his toes, which I later dug out with a nail file. Three of the cats had to be put in a box to catch the bus home, but Cubby just let me pick him up and walk him to the bus stop, where he sat on the bench with us without a leash. Apparently, he'd been so miserable in that shop that he just saw us as his liberators or something. I applied the socializing process that I give every cat, but Cub and I grew closer and closer as he did stuff like pawing me on the face to wake me every morning. An interesting thing about Cub is his unusual thoughtfulness. While other cats around here act on impulse, Cub always seems to stop, consider his actions, and then continue. He's never caused me any kind of grief or goofy antics

like other cats. We're now pretty much at the telepathic
level of communication.

His story was so compelling I didn't want him to stop. I felt I had
just touched the surface of all that Patrick had to say. With just
another question, he gladly went on:

From my earliest years, I liked to paint pictures; one of my very first
memories is of being in trouble for using bedsheets as canvas to
paint on. For some reason, I really liked to draw cats as early as five
years old. Also, I'd spend every summer three months a year at my
grandparents' farm in the country. They grew produce organically
using cow manure. In those days (and I'm told this still happens),
it was common for a farm to have ten, even thirty cats, as folks
weren't aware of spaying/neutering like today. My grandfather
never drowned kittens in front of me, but I knew about it and
thought it very disturbing. That probably had something to do
with what I do today. They had around twenty cats on the farm,
which were fed mostly scraps and fresh cow's milk, and yes, my
grandparents could squirt milk into a cat's mouth while milking
a cow and the whole farm cat bit. I had no social life with other
kids during stays at the farm. Since I liked to draw cats, I spent
lots of time with the cats at the large shed they'd staked in several
different territories. These weren't feral cats; they hung out with
humans but had all manner of semiwild behavior and social
structures you don't see often today, such as unneutered males
killing litters of kittens fathered by males other than themselves,
lots of fights, and nighttime rumbles. I was always very intuitive but
also good at scientific observation. I had three favorite cats that
I bonded with in particular: Blimp, a giant, fat, mean, and nasty
cowcat tom; Hitler, another black-and-white cowcat so named
because his markings made him look like Der Fuehrer; and Henry
Cabot Lodge, whom my right-wing grandparents had affectionately
named after one of the founders of the Republican Party. Blimp
was the alpha king cat because of his size and mean-spiritedness. It
was with these cats that I first, around age nine, developed the cat
communication methods I teach to people at the market today: If
you build a structure where cats can be up higher than you when
they want to, looking down at your face instead of being on the

ground looking up at your knees, the cats feel more powerful; Even wildcats can sometimes be "reached"; Cats always respond immediately to extra attention; You can put several sentences of information into one simple hand gesture that the cat understands much more readily than spoken words. And feeding the cat's ego and self-centeredness is ironically the key to getting them to do what you want: you have to give them a reason to be interested in what you want.

One of the things Patrick loves about his visits to Pike Place Market is getting to meet and talk to other cat lovers. As a cat lover myself, I understand his desire to meet with others who feel like we do. We may have very different cultural values and may not even speak the same language, but cat lovers will find a way to communicate and connect with other cat lovers. Most of us are quick to pull out photographs of our cats, which we proudly show off. We can spend hours exchanging cat stories, from the mundane to the extraordinary. It can also become an opportunity to share information on everything, from herbal remedies to brands of cat food. It is emotionally gratifying to talk to others who "get" it.

Patrick and I get each other, and I am so happy that I decided to stop and talk to him on my trip to Seattle this time. I've already learned so much from him about cat communication, and it's only the beginning. Our friendship has just begun.

Famous Painters and Cats

Cats have captured the imagination of some very famous painters who went on to paint them in oils, pastels, watercolors, and on posters.

The French artist Pierre Renoir loved cats and depicted them in several paintings.

Théophile Steinlen, a Swiss artist, was yet another artist who often depicted cats in his work. His Paris home was in fact known as the CatsCorner.

Alessandra and Tiffany

The Atlantic is not as big as it looks, not when you're a cat lover.

I have never met my Italian cousin, Alessandra. Our mothers, who are first cousins, grew up next door to each other in a tiny mountainside village near Rome. To this day, they remain as close as sisters even though they are half a world away from each other. When my mother came to this country at age 15, she left Alessandra's mother behind, but they have kept in constant contact via telephone. Growing up, I had often heard of my little cousin and she of me; but she has never been in the United States, and I have never been to Italy. Yet we share a bond as our mothers do, only in a more modern sense: via the Internet.

With every e-mail that we exchange, I find myself thinking of her life in Italy. On the surface, we are very different: Alessandra is an attorney, single, and lives with her mother. I am ten years older than she is, a veterinary technician, married with two teenaged boys. Her life is filled with trips up the coast heading to Tuscany for the day, shopping in the finest stores of Rome, and dancing the night away in an Italian discotheque in Abruzzo.

She loves all things American, even the classic movies. In fact, she named her cat, Tiffany, after the famous film *Breakfast at Tiffany's*, written by Truman Capote, a cat lover. I love all things Italian, and the older I get, the more I appreciate my heritage. I shop for Italian gold online, treasure my Italian silk scarf and Venetian glass heart necklace. Every year, we vacation at Villa Roma, a resort in the Catskills Mountains of New York, where most of the boys are named Anthony. It's the closest I've come to actually being in Italy.

My cousin and I have built a strong e-mail relationship over the past few years. She insists that we write in English to strengthen her English skills, for which I am ever grateful since my Italian is rusty at best. The more we e-mailed, the more we realized that maybe we weren't so different after all. We discovered that what we had most in common was our complete craziness and love for cats. Our electronic messages went back and forth between Italy and Brookfield, Connecticut, where we shared stories and downloaded pictures of our beloved felines.

> Cara Cugina,
> Today mama and I took a ride to Tuscany. Tiffany came along with us; she loves to ride in the car. When we got there, we stopped at the most beautiful little bistro and had cappuccino and biscotti. Tiffany had latte, or as you say, milk! It was a glorious day.

Tiffany

> Cara Alessandra,
> Your rides to Tuscany make me jealous. I can just imagine the three of you riding up the coast with the wind in your hair. One day, I will join you and you can show me all of the sites of Italy.

Carrrrrrrrttyytyswrtghbneima Cugiieeeeeeegnvna,
As you can seeeeeeeeeeee, Tiffany is helping me type this
email to you.
She had become quite the keeyyyyyyybboaarderrrrrrrr
rrrrrrr you know.

She sends baci!

Our cats also live very different lives. While Rhiannon basks in the sunlight of my sunroom just off my kitchen, Tiffany rolls and stretches in the garden of the summer home in our family's hometown. As TiVo drinks the water faucet at my kitchen sink, Tiffany is playing with the garden hose among the tomatoes, basil, and peppers that grow there. Each cat lives an idyllic life no matter which side of the Atlantic you view it from.

With each e-mail that was exchanged between us, I began to think what my life would have been like in Italy had my parents never come to this country. As Alessandra would describe the rolling hills of Abruzzo, the hustle and bustle of Rome, and weekend trips to Tuscany, I would imagine her life as my own. Through her words on my computer screen, I could visualize cruising up the Italian coastline with Tiffany by my side, the wind blowing through my long auburn hair. I could hear the strings of Old World Italian music, and I could almost smell the ocean. How wonderfully romantic it must be. She said she would also think of me, her cousin on the East Coast of the United States. I told her of the beautiful autumn colors, the sleeplessness of New York City, and our own rolling hills of Litchfield, Connecticut.

But her happy e-mails took on an urgent tone in the spring of 2008. Alessandra was afraid that Tiffany was dying.

Cara Cugina,
I am afraid that this letter to you is not a happy one. I am so worried about my Tiffany. She will not eat; she has not touched her food in 2 days. She will do nothing but stay all curled up in the corner of my bedroom. I

called my veterinarian, but he is away on vacation for 10 days. He is a mobile vet that makes house calls. I cannot take her to another vet because she is a difficult patient and gets agitated when I bring her to the office. The other vets in the practice will not see her because of her aggression. I don't know what to do. Please . . . tell me what I should do.

From across the ocean, I had to help my cousin and her cat Tiffany, a cat I knew so well she felt like one of my own.

Dear Alessandra,
It is not good when a cat stops eating. It is a sure sign that something is not well. Are you certain that no one will see Tiffany? She needs help now, not in ten days. From what you are telling me I urge you to find someone who will see her. Is she vomiting? Is she going to the litter box? Has she ever been sick like this before?

Cara Cugina,
She has always been a healthy cat. When we got her as a kitten 10 years ago she was a little small but she quickly gained weight and has always been a good eater. I do not know what to do. I wish that you lived in Italy. I am so worried. She will eat nothing that I give her. I tried everything. And yes, she is also begun to vomit, even though she isn't eating. It's clear liquid.

Cara Alessandra,
I understand what it is like to have an aggressive cat in the office and I can understand why you would want to wait for your mobile vet to come back from vacation but Tiffany needs to be seen by a vet now. Please try to find someone who will see her. From what you are telling me she may have an obstruction of her intestines and that is an emergency. I don't want to scare you, but please go for help right away.

The e-mails continued from Rome:

> Cugina Carisima,
> I called another veterinarian who has agreed to see her
> and I am bringing her over right now. Thank you so
> much and please, pray for her. As you can imagine it's
> not a good time for our family. I know there are a lot of
> ill people, children included, who are suffering all over
> the world, but it's hard seeing this little creature we love
> so much in this condition and I'm writing to you because
> I know you can understand. Forgive my English today, it's
> very bad! I hope that my next communication with you
> will be a happy one. I am so scared.

Two days went by, and there was nothing from Rome. Finally, on
the third day, there she was in my in-box:

> Cara Cugina,
> I am sorry that I have not written to you in a few days. I've
> been so upset about Tiffany. I'm so glad you told me this
> was an emergency because as it turns out, the veterinarian
> took an x-ray and found that she was obstructed with
> what looks like a string type of material. I cannot imagine
> what this might be. I do not have any string in my house.
> This was the reason she was not eating. She is scheduled
> for surgery this afternoon. I am so nervous. I will let you
> know what happens.

The waiting on this side of the Atlantic felt like an eternity. I can
only imagine what it felt like to my cousin. As each hour passed by
with no word in my in-box, I began to fear the worst. I checked my
e-mail one last time that evening before heading to bed, still no
word from Rome. I tossed and turned all night, barely getting any
sleep. The next morning, through my very sleepy eyes, I saw it:

> Cara Cugina bellissima,
> I don't know how I can ever thank you enough. If I had
> waited until my veterinarian returned, Tiffany would no

longer be with me. The surgery to remove the obstruction was successful and she is recovering well. He took out dental floss. Who would think that dental floss could possibly kill my beautiful girl? I know that she tries to go into the garbage in my bathroom and pull things out to play with but I never even thought that something so benign could hurt her in any way. I guess I have to be more careful with my curious little Tiffany. I will bring her home later this afternoon. The veterinarian said that she would be fine.

Carissima Alessandra,
Dental floss, Christmas tree tinsel, Easter grass, ribbon, thread . . . all of these things could be lethal to a cat, as you now know. I am so glad that Tiffany will be fine. I am not sure what could have made me happier than to see your wonderful news. I am ecstatic that I have helped you in some way even though we are thousands of miles apart. I cannot stop smiling. I read your e-mail through tears of joy. Please give Tiffany a big kiss from her cousin in America.

The next day, I received another happy e-mail from Rome.

Cugina Mia, GRAZIE! Tiffany is home with me and she is already eating again. Mama and I are as you say in America "Over the Moon!" Tiffany wanted me to send you a big Italian kitty kiss. Baci baci baci!

I realized that our very different lives are not so different after all. My cousin and I share a special relationship, and we have never met. We understand each other, and we have never spoken. We love each other and have never even hugged. Our family ties have brought us together, but it is our love for cats that has truly connected us. With each e-mail, our bond gets stronger and stronger.

The world has become a very small place. How fortunate we both are that Italy is just a mouse click away from Connecticut.

Tiffany

Cats and the Reign of Terror

The Reign of Terror occurred after the French Revolution in the late 1700s. Perhaps the most symbolic execution was that of Marie Antoinette by the guillotine. However, humans were not the only victims during the Reign of Terror.

Cats, which had been worshipped by the ancient Egyptians, were now being persecuted. The earliest record of such persecution occurred during a ceremony known as Cat Wednesday in the city of Metz in northern France. Hundreds of cats were burned alive in the belief that they were witches in disguise.

Cats would once again regain their proper status in Europe, but it took over one hundred years to get there.

Lin and Her Siamese Cats

Lin needs to take care of cats. It is as much a necessity for her as breathing. I've met a lot of people who want to help cats. Some volunteer their time at shelters, others provide foster care for cats, but no one is like Lin.

I first met Lin when she dropped off her business card at the clinic. At fifty-nine, she had just started a cat nanny service and thought a cat-only hospital would be a perfect place for referrals. And of course, she was right. As chance would have it, the following week, a receptionist position opened up. Linda, waving Lin's card in front of me, suggested I call her. A phone call and an interview later, I had a new employee. I didn't know much about her. She was a very private person, but I sensed right away her connection to cats. Within a day, she knew all the resident clinic cats by name, which is quite impressive as there are more than I am willing to admit to. Within a week, she knew all their unique personalities and was tending to them as if they were her own. Every morning, I would hear her chatting away with the cats; sometimes she would even sing to them. They would all get an equal amount of her attention; she played no favorites here. Lin fit in so well that it felt like she had been at the clinic forever.

As if all this cat care weren't enough, after a full day at the clinic, she had her cat nanny business to attend to. Off to somebody else's home she would go to take care of those cats too. From there she would finally head home and take care of her own two Siamese cats. From morning till night, a good part of every day for Lin was taking care of cats. She had such an uncanny and profound connection to them all that I began to call her the cat whisperer.

One day, Lin and I were the only two working at the clinic, and I took the opportunity to chat with her privately. I was hoping to learn a little more about her. The conversation started naturally enough: where do you come from, any brothers or sisters, the usual small talk in getting to know one another on a deeper level. I'll never know why, but for some reason, on that day, Lin opened up and shared a very painful part of her childhood.

She grew up in rural upstate New York. The house she lived in was a two-story white colonial that her maternal grandfather built. It had a big front porch where they would often sit, drink lemonade and iced tea, and watch the cars go by. Attached was a huge garage that was bigger than the house itself. From the outside, it looked idyllic. But the road claimed many a careless cat, and the house proved to have its tragedies as well.

Her parents, Doris and Austen, had a difficult marriage. Her father, although not physically abusive, was a very dominant man with a rigid personality. Her mother suffered from depression at a time when little was understood about this disease. Her depression went completely untreated. Doris often packed a suitcase, and Lin was left to wonder why and where she was going. There was always the nagging fear that her mother would just disappear one day, perhaps into thin air.

Lin was left alone much of her childhood to fend for herself. Her parents were too busy taking care of themselves to properly take care of their only child.

"I was very lonely when I was a little girl," she told me in her delicate childlike voice. "The cats were my constant companions. They were my friends and my playmates. I remember Tuffy and Timmy the most, especially Tuffy. With his long brown tabby coat, he was just beautiful. He followed me around everywhere I went, in the house and outside too. I used to dress him in my doll clothes, put him in the stroller, and push him around the house. I really loved him and needed him. Yes, the cats were everything to me."

When Lin was nine years old, her mother brought home two seal point Siamese kittens. With their constant jabbering and mischievousness, they brought much needed joy to the house. Their names were Mickey and Brownie. Because they lived on a busy road, these cats were going to be kept indoors. However, her mom wanted them to enjoy the outside world a little, so she bought special leashes for them and set up an outside run. These cats had a great life, indoors and out. Everybody in the house simply adored them.

For the next two years, things seemed to go smoothly enough. Although her mom's depression still permeated the house, Lin found ways to be happy and fill her days. There was school, homework, chores, and of course, Mickey and Brownie. Then the unthinkable happened. Lin was only eleven years old. Her mom came into her room and said the last words she would ever say to her: "Lin, take care of the cats."

With that, she left the room and went into the den. The next thing Lin heard was a gunshot. Lin ran into the room and was the first to find her mother. Doris had committed suicide by shooting herself in the chest. That moment would haunt Lin for the rest of her life.

I now understood the sadness I sometimes saw in Lin's eyes. It hasn't been an easy life for her. How could it be? She's married and divorced a couple of times, has suffered with her own anxiety and depression. Throughout it all, there are the cats in her life. They not only continue to be joyful companions, but they also keep her grounded to the earth.

"There was Sam," she smiled remembering him. "I called him a Siamese fraud because he was only half-Siamese. We had this wooden canoe that my grandfather built, and Sam would come canoeing with me. He was there through the worst of my divorce too. He wasn't just my companion. He was like a limb, an arm or a leg."

Sam on the canoe

Lin has two Siamese cats in her life again, Sammy and Simba, whom she dotes on constantly. She also has a wonderful husband, Jeff, who dotes on her. What started out as a simple getting-to-know-you conversation turned into a turning point in our friendship and in my understanding of the cat whisperer that is Lin. I now understand the beauty of her relationship with cats. She needs to take care of them, and in return, they take care of her.

Lin recently found out that the huge garage of the white colonial house she grew up in is now a veterinary hospital. We both decided that her mother's ghost must still be there, making sure cats get taken care of everywhere.

Lin and her Siamese cats

One Hundred Breeds of Cat

Whereas once there was only one type of cat, the domestic cat, there are now one hundred specific breeds of cats. In the pursuit to perpetuate the beauty and elegance of specific breeds, cat lovers continue to improve upon already established breeds and sometimes create new ones. Breeders work toward improving not only the looks of a breed but also their temperament and health as well. This helps pet owners decide which cat is the best fit for their family.

The very first official breeds of cat are thought to be the Egyptian Mau and the Abyssinian. Both have the intermediate body structure and wedge-shaped head with the facial structure of the African wildcat. Some other of the most popular breeds are the American Curl, American Shorthair, British Shorthair, Bombay, Chartreux, Maine Coon, Persian, Russian Blue, and Siamese.

With one hundred breeds to choose from, anyone can find the cat of his or her dreams.

John and Rosemary Goudy and the Cats of Goudy Lane

Reality TV takes a whole new meaning in the lives of John and Rosemary Goudy. They may seem like your typical retired couple, but there's a lot more to them than days in the garden or crossword puzzles. We first met them in the summer of 2000.

"This is Wingnut, my wife and I noticed him on our surveillance camera," John Goudy announced as he walked through the front door of the clinic.

Wingnut? Surveillance camera? What?

When I looked up from the reception desk, I saw a very handsome older couple. Mr. Goudy was well dressed; in fact, he was in a suit and tie. With his finely chiseled features and wrinkle-free face, he looked much younger than his seventy years. His wife, Rosemary, was a small soft-spoken woman with porcelain skin and soft blond hair. This was hardly a couple who would name their cat Wingnut, I thought. Or was it?

I was intrigued to learn more. After all, there had to be a pretty good story behind that name. I ushered them into the exam room where Dr. Eisen would be examining the cat. When I asked for a history on the cat, it became clear who the talker in this family was. Rosemary stood by and quietly watched the man that she'd been with for fifty years tell their story.

"We don't let this get around much, but you're cat people, you'll understand." And John began to tell us all about the mysterious and unusual way they spend their days.

He told us all about the video cameras that are set up to view every angle of their backyard. They had installed top-of-the-line surveillance equipment that captured every moment of the night. Dr. Eisen and I looked at each other in disbelief. After all, who would do such a thing? And why?

There have been all sorts of animals that have come in and out of their yard, they continued, but they are most fascinated by the nocturnal world of the feral cat. They explained how each of their cats had come into their lives. Wingnut was quite cautious as he made his way through the deep woods of the back of the yard. Step by step he moved closer to the house. The cameras scanned his every move. For days, they would watch as he inched closer and closer to the house. We were so caught up in his story it was like watching a movie. I almost asked Dr. Eisen to pass the popcorn. Slowly but surely, Wingnut made his way toward the back door of the house. They saw him actually try to eat plumbing supplies. So *that's* how he got his name.

"Yeah, he figured out pretty quickly that Fancy Feast tasted much better than metal," John said with that sparkle in his eyes and dry wit that we have come to know so well.

The Goudys live in a large, stately house, which John is quick to point out "would make a great funeral home." Behind it, the stage is set for reality television at its best. At the far end of the yard, there are many tall oak and maple trees, with scattered blue spruce trees here and there. Even in the hot humid summers of the Northeast, it remains cool in this part of the yard because of the greenery. Wildflowers line the edges of the property, and a large white gazebo graces the middle of the yard. Adjacent to the house is a large patio with a small pond. Look closely and you'll see the cameras in every corner as they catch every episode of Goudy TV.

"The first time we saw Dumpster, she fell into the pond. We figured we'd have to invest in feline scuba lessons or maybe try to get her to live inside our house," John told us with a wry smile. This lucky cat started out homeless with an affinity for their garbage cans, on top of which she spent most of her nights. Elegant Dumpster now lives the good life and spends most of her days preening her soft silver fur in the sunshine of their living room bay window.

Each time they came to the clinic, they had more stories about what the cameras had captured during the night. While other people their age may wile away the hours with *The Price Is Right* or *Judge Judy*, John and Rosemary have their own version of Animal Planet going on. Every morning, while Rosemary brews coffee and prepares breakfast, John retrieves the tapes and rewinds them for the morning entertainment. The TV schedule has so much to choose from. There's *Meal or No Meal* with Meowie Mandel, *Nine Lives To Live*, the fine queens of *The Meow*, and the riveting *Adventures of Black Bart*.

Who is Black Bart? you ask. We asked the same question. Naturally, he had his very own story. In his first appearance, Black Bart meandered straight up to a huge raccoon, looked him up and down as if to say, "You're not so bad, tough guy, I could take you." He then walked right past this animal who was twice his size and headed for the cat food that was set up at the back door. Just before he put his head down to eat from the bowl, he looked at the raccoon and gave him a slow and subtle "hhhiiiisssssss." The raccoon turned his tail and ran away. You could almost hear the old Western music on the tape. From that moment on, he claimed the Goudys' patio as his territory, and no one dared cross his path. With a glare or a hiss, the other animals learned to respect Black Bart.

There was a new sheriff in town.

Black Bart

Every night the cameras captured new episodes of Black Bart and his kingdom. Then one day, the inevitable happened. Someone got the better of ole Bart. As the Goudys watched their tape, they could see he was hurt. His soft onyx fur was bloodied and matted. His usual confident stroll was now a painful limp. They managed to trap him and quickly got him to the clinic. As they brought him through the door, they announced his arrival. We brought him to the back room, away from the prying eyes of the paparazzi (well, all right, maybe it was the cats that live at the clinic). As I held him on the exam table, it was as though I was meeting a Hollywood star. I had heard so much about him. To me, he was legendary; and there he was, disheveled, frail, defeated. But as I looked at his big golden eyes, he looked straight at mine as if to say, "You should see the other guy." We cleaned his wounds, stitched him up, and neutered him. Black Bart got a lot more than he bargained for that day. When they took him home later that afternoon, they tried to keep him inside. But he would have none of that. Only a few days later, he made his escape. The back door was left slightly ajar, and he ran out. Black Bart was not a cat that could be confined. His indoor days were over. And besides, how could he possibly live in a house with cats named Wingnut or Dumpster?

With each new character that entered, the Goudys did their best to help. Because of them, many neighborhood strays were fed, spayed or neutered, and given the proper vaccines. The Goudys have a comfortable retirement, and they are more than willing to spend their time and money taking care of the cats on Goudy Lane. To them, any cat is worth the trouble, even the most homely. But that's not where all their money goes.

One of John's indulgences is a small collection of luxury cars. When Dr. Eisen's beautiful lilac British Shorthair, Bentley, was called for a photo shoot for a television commercial, she phoned John to ask him if he could bring one of his cars to the clinic so that Bentley could be photographed on *his* Bentley. John had the car washed and waxed and drove it up to the clinic, where he insisted that the cat be placed directly on the car and not on the towel that Dr. Eisen placed upon it so he wouldn't scratch its fine paint.

John insisted that the towel would ruin the picture. He didn't care about damaging the car; he cared about her cat and the photo shoot. Dr. Eisen couldn't bear the thought of scratching the car, and the towel ended up in the shoot. Bentley did not get the gig, but that picture remains one of our most prized possessions.

As we've grown so fond of this wonderful couple, another wrench (no, that's not the name of one of their cats) has been thrown into the plans. Since moving to Connecticut over forty-five years ago, they always dreamed that one day, they would move back to their hometown in Minnesota. They are now realizing that dream and have put their home on the market. But it's not so simple.

What will happen to the feral cats of Clapboard Ridge Road?

Who will buy a house that looks like a funeral home and has video surveillance cameras covering every angle of the backyard?

Will Black Bart change his name to Minnesota Cat?

These questions and more will be answered in the next season of Goudy TV.

Talk about a cliff-hanger!

Felix the Cat

With his black body, giant eyes, and wide grin, Felix the cat became one of the most famous cartoon cats in the world. He is best described by his theme song, which is as follows:

> He's amazing, he's remarkable
> He is fearless, unbelievable
> He is superdooper and extraordinary
> He's the kind of guy that keeps you feeling merry
> Who?
>
> Felix the cat
> The wonderful, wonderful cat
> Whenever he gets in a fix
> He reaches into his bag of tricks
>
> Felix the cat
> The wonderful, wonderful cat
> You'll laugh so much your sides will ache
> Your heart will go pit-a-pat
> Watching Felix the wonderful cat[*]

Although he was created in the silent movie era, he lives on in many forms of memorabilia, which people collect to this very day.

---

[*]   http://www.justsomelyrics.com/1199243/TV-Themes-Felix-The-Cat-Lyrics

Pat and Chloe

Pat Herrington believes a kitten saved her life. We first met Pat when she came to see our British Shorthair kittens. She had decided to adopt one after seeing them on our Web site. Pat was healthy then, or so she thought.

We led her to the kitten room, and within seconds, she was down on the floor at their level. It didn't matter that her blond hair was perfectly coiffed or that she was still in her freshly dry-cleaned clothes, if getting a sense of the kittens meant crawling around the fur-laden rug, then so be it.

"That's her," she said excitedly. "The blue-and-white one looking at me from the corner. I want her."

She had chosen a shy little girl with a pair of big round eyes that could melt the iciest of hearts. Pat couldn't tell us exactly why, but she sensed something about this kitten. She had to have her. Since the kittens were only two weeks old, Pat had another six weeks to wait before she could take her home.

"That's okay," she said. "We have years and years ahead of us. It'll be a long six weeks, but I'll come by every week to visit her. And by the way, her name is Chloe." With that, she kissed her Chloe, picked herself up off the floor, brushed herself off, and said good-bye.

The following week, camera in hand, Pat was at the clinic to visit us. She was on the floor again, this time taking pictures of her perfect kitten. Before she left, she confided to us that she would be having some minor surgery to correct an annoying and somewhat embarrassing problem. She assured us it was no big deal and that she would be back the following week to spend time with Chloe.

These visits were important for both of them, she told us, and she didn't intend to miss a single opportunity for their bonding to continue. In the meanwhile, Linda and I were doing our own bonding with Pat.

Right on schedule, Pat was at the clinic for her next weekly visit. We could see she was not herself. It wasn't easy for her to tell us what was wrong; it was such an embarrassing thing to talk about. Pat had gone to correct what the doctor thought was a nagging hemorrhoid, but instead he found a large cancerous tumor in her rectum. She would be going in for further surgery to remove the tumor and surrounding lymph nodes. Her doctors said her prognosis was good, but still, it was devastating.

"And I'm such a priss. Of all people to get rectal cancer, it had to be me!" she joked.

This time, when she went to visit Chloe, it took on a whole new meaning. Chloe was becoming her therapy, a time to forget, if only for a few moments, what lay ahead for her.

Pat had the surgery just a few short days after her visit with us. The tumor, it turned out, was bigger than they had anticipated; and they couldn't remove it all. She would need radiation and chemotherapy to kill the remaining cancer. That could be done on an outpatient basis, and she assured us that she would not miss her visits with Chloe. In fact, she needed them now more than ever. The pictures she had been collecting through the weeks were on her computer, and her favorite picture had become her screen saver. Whenever she needed a lift, she had only to turn on her computer and see Chloe's big soulful eyes looking at her.

Visits became harder as the weeks progressed. The treatments were taking a toll on her health and her spirit. She needed help with everything, including getting to the clinic. Her mother began to accompany her to the office. Pat was getting weaker and weaker. On one of her visits, she had to hold on to the wall as she made her way to the room where Chloe was. She lost her hair, wore a kerchief; it was heartbreaking to see her like that.

"I needed to see my kitten," she told us. "I would look at Chloe, and I knew she was having an effect on my body. I know it sounds metaphysical, but it's the only way I can describe it. Being with her, touching her, was giving me the energy that the treatments were taking away."

The week before Pat was to take her kitten home, she didn't show up. We were very worried. We knew how important these visits had become and understood what her not coming might mean. Every day that passed without hearing from Pat made us more concerned. The week went by, and the day Pat was to take Chloe home arrived. We still had not heard from her. We began to fear the worst. We called her home; no answer. I had the idea to call the hospital where she had told us she was getting her treatments and finally found her. She was able to answer the phone but sounded awful. She barely had the strength to speak. There were complications from the treatments; her intestines had become obstructed, and she had had emergency surgery to clear her bowels. She had no idea when she would be well enough to go home. In fact, she confided, she had almost died. She sounded very depressed. Pat, the woman who never missed a chance to see her kitten, who was always so upbeat, who was so certain she could beat his thing, had the voice of defeat.

Pat sounded so terrible that we both felt we needed to do something to help her, and we needed to do it that very day. I told Linda to call the nurses' station to ask if we could bring Chloe to the hospital. The nurses loved the idea. They had seen Chloe's photograph next to Pat's hospital bed and understood how much this little kitten meant to her. Linda gave me the thumb's up. We loaded Chloe into the car and, with fearful excitement, made our way to the hospital. It felt like we were bringing vital medicine to a critical patient.

We entered the hospital with our precious surprise in hand. The nurses, after oohing and aahing at the kitten, directed us to Pat's room. We entered quietly, holding Chloe in our arms. Pat was in a hospital gown, attached to an IV pole, and barely able to hold herself up in the chair. She looked terrible. When she first looked up, she didn't realize who we were. Then she saw Chloe, and her whole demeanor changed in an instant. The biggest smile crossed her face, and the tears began to fall. She held her arms up, and we placed Chloe in them, where she belonged. Chloe truly was the best medicine.

Pat and Chloe

Three days later, Pat left the hospital. The following day, she came for Chloe and took her home.

Chloe has since celebrated her first birthday, and Pat a year of being cancer free. She comes to the clinic often, sometimes with Chloe, sometimes just to say hi and tell us about what is going on in her life. Because of this experience, she has decided to go into "healing touch" therapy and is on her way to becoming certified. She tells us about Chloe's aura, which is very large. Perhaps that is what attracted her to this kitten from the very beginning? Being a believer in traditional medicine, I am very skeptical of nontraditional treatments. But in this case, I too believe that a kitten saved Pat's life.

As a special birthday gift to Chloe and in celebration of the many years they will share together, Pat gave her a baby brother, Shiloh.

Shiloh

Cats the Musical

In 1981, *Cats* the musical debuted in the West End in London and, one year later, opened on Broadway in New York. In London, the musical ran for twenty-one years, and on Broadway, for eighteen years, both setting records of long runs. *Cats* has been performed around the world and has been translated into twenty different languages.

Composed by Frank Lloyd Webber and based on the book, *Old Possum's Book of Practical Cats* by T. S. Eliot, *Cats* has become a classic musical production with some of the most beloved characters and songs. There is Mr. Mistoffelees, a young tom with magical powers; Griddlebone, a fluffy white Persian; and Grizabella, a former glamour cat, among many other cat characters.

Awards include Best New Musical in the Tony Awards and Olivier Awards.

Cats, the musical, is a testament to the enduring love of cats by artists, composers, singers, actors, and patrons.

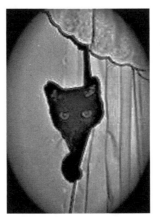

Cindy Chen and the Shelter Cats

We knew that Cindy Chen worked at the local animal shelter, but beyond that, we didn't know anything about her. A client had mentioned her as someone we could call if we had any extra food, litter, or other supplies we wanted to donate to the shelter. "Just call Cindy," she said, "and she'll be over lickety-split." Indeed, after a call to her, Cindy would show up within a couple of hours, cordially greet us, thank us, and be on her way. She wasn't a person that would dillydally or make small talk, like many other people do. On occasion, we would try to engage her in conversation, but we never succeeded in getting her relaxed. To confess, we all thought of her as nice but a bit boring.

"What do you think she does at the shelter?" Sharon asked me one day as we watched Cindy drive away.

"I don't know. Maybe she takes inventory of the food?" Linda replied.

"I think she may be the office manager. She just looks the type," Lin, our receptionist, added.

We knew Cindy was of Asian descent; we could tell that from her physical appearance, and we knew that she was devoted to the shelter. But beyond the obvious, we knew nothing. Was there anything else to know?

One day, Cindy walked in just as we sat down for morning coffee, an indulgent ritual at the clinic. We sit around and catch up on what's new in our lives, what's good on television, or what movies we might recommend to each other. Cindy was on her way to pick up another bag of cat food for the shelter cats.

"Let's invite her to have coffee with us," I said to Dr. Eisen.

"Good idea," she replied.

"Come sit with us, Cindy," I asked.

She was very reluctant, but with a little encouragement, she timidly sat down. We started asking her questions about her background. She was not much of a talker, and it was clear that she felt uncomfortable talking about herself. This wasn't going to be easy, for her or for us.

She began by telling us that she was born in China and raised in Taiwan. She came to America in 1965, when she was twenty-four years old, leaving her family and friends behind. Cindy didn't show much emotion, but we imagined that it must have been a very difficult time of her life. She went to the University of Utah, received her MBA, got married, and had a son. The family then settled in the Danbury, Connecticut, area where Cindy worked in her profession for many years.

Most people, when asked to talk about themselves, will happily go on and on. But not Cindy. She was terse and to the point. No nonsense here. No playfulness either. Perhaps even a bit dull, we all thought.

She shifted in the chair, finished her coffee, and set her mug down on the countertop. She was about ready to flee her discomfort when one of our most shy house cats, Sabrina, jumped up onto her lap. We all thought it strange that of all cats to approach Cindy, it was Sabrina. She didn't like anyone. Cindy looked more comfortable as she gently stroked Sabrina, so we took the opportunity to ask her what it was she actually did at the shelter. With the cat in her lap, Cindy began to relax. She was even bold enough to ask for a second cup of coffee. "I thought that I would enjoy early retirement," she began," but something was missing from my life."

She had always loved cats. As a little girl growing up in Taiwan, her family had two cats that she had many fond memories of. When the local animal shelter was looking for volunteers, she answered the call. There were others to help with the animals and to deal with the prospective adoptive families, but with her background in accounting, she felt that was where she could help the most. Three times a week, she gave two hours to the shelter doing their bookkeeping.

Since her office was in the rear of the shelter, she had to walk by the cages where the cats were housed. She would look at their lonely, frightened faces and feel particularly sad for the ones that were there the longest and never got adopted. Cats could end up in the shelter for months because they were "unadoptable" due to their temperaments. The aggressive ones, the shyest ones, the older ones—they were the ones that she saw week after week, month after month.

One night, Cindy changed her normal routine, and it was this one small change that changed everything. Instead of simply walking by all the cages, she stopped, opened a cage, took a cat out, and brought him to her office. His name was Oliver. All the cats at the shelter are given names. It's one small way of making the cats seem more like family than a detainee. Oliver had been there for months, but everyone who came to adopt passed him by. He was a particularly nervous and untrusting cat. If you approached him, he would either cower in the back of the cage or lunge at you. Everyone thought of him as a hopeless case.

In his first visit to the office, he spent the entire time under Cindy's desk. Cindy paid little attention to him; she just went about her business, and every so often, she would look under the desk and talk to him in a calm, reassuring voice. When it was time for Cindy to leave, she returned him to his cage, wished him a good night and went home. This went on for several weeks until, one day, Oliver came out from under the desk and began to curiously walk around the office. With her quiet, patient manner, Cindy slowly but surely gained the trust of this cat. Oliver was never what you might call outgoing, but he went from a hisser to a cat that was able to purr. He was adoptable.

Cindy had discovered her niche. Oliver was just the beginning. Fluffy was next, Dexter followed, and one by one, these "hopeless" cats began to find homes of their own. Cindy not only did their bookkeeping, but also became the on-call cat whisperer.

We asked Cindy how it felt after these cats were adopted. Did she miss them? Did she feel a sense of loss?

"I don't feel like I am losing them. I am happy for them. Many people feel like their cats are their children, but I don't see them this way. I see them as my equals," Cindy explained. "The sole reason for me to make the bond is for them to be adopted. When I achieve that, that's my accomplishment."

If the cats at the animal shelter could talk and we had asked them about Cindy Chen, they would have painted a very different picture of the person we thought she was. Snug and warm in the love of their new adopted families, they'll tell you how Cindy Chen taught them how to trust again and how to be comfortable in their own fur.

And what about Oliver? He's the one that started the whole process. Whatever happened to him?

"Oh, he has a wonderful life now. He lives in a big house in Danbury." She smiled. "He lives with me."

Since that day, when we finally got to know the real Cindy, she has come to the clinic many times to pick up supplies for the shelter. She still doesn't say much, still quietly picks up the supplies, thanks us, and returns to the shelter. But now, we know that Cindy truly is one of the unsung heroes in the cat world.

Cindy Chen at the office picking up food for the shelter

The Hemingway Cats

Ernest Hemingway, the famous author, was also a passionate cat lover. He admired their spirit and independence. While living in Key West, Florida, he acquired his very first cat from a ship captain. The cat was probably a Maine Coon cat because it was polydactyl (Latin for "many digits"). The trait for polydactylism is a dominant gene; therefore, the offspring of this cat are also multitoed. As a result of this, the polydactyl cats of the world are also known as Hemingway cats.

The home in Key West is now a museum and a sanctuary for the descendants of the cats that Ernest Hemingway originally and lovingly adopted. His estate was willed to his beloved cats, and people come from far and wide just to see them. Today there are approximately sixty cats living there, and half of them have those Hemingway toes.

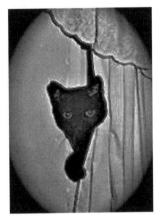

Breanne and Murray

Murray was one of the most memorable cats I have ever met. Born without a tail, he seemed unfinished in a way. But as fate would have it, someone named Breanne fell in love with him, and where he ended, she began.

Breanne told me it was love at first sight. Cupid's arrow struck her on September 30, 2003. Her cousin had found a little kitten and, knowing Breanne was a cat lover, invited her over to meet him. The moment she laid eyes on him, she knew he would be going home with her.

When I asked her what it was about him that made him so irresistible, she said, "It was his rear end. He had no tail, and he was just so cute without it. I loved his impish face, and when he looked at me, I knew he was trouble. I could tell he had a great personality because even though he was still just a little kitten, he was rolling and licking and playing with the big dogs in the house. He knew how to hold his ground, and I knew I would be taking him home."

Breanne took him home that very day, and the love between them only grew and got stronger. Murray, it turns out, was a most unusual cat.

"Murray loved to be vacuumed," she told me with pride. "I don't know why, but he just loved it. He could hear me turn on the vacuum anywhere in the house, and he would come running. I would run the vacuum over his body, and he would sit there and purr and coo. He also loved all animals. We had a hamster, and he would sit and stare at him all the time. He even loved Fluffy, our parakeet. He would rub his body up against him. And he loved to get into boxes, the smaller the better. He would wedge himself into the tiniest box. He ate dinner with us too. He had his place at the table, right between my mom and me. Best of all, he always waited for me at the door when I came home. We always had our time together, where we would sit and cuddle. He was just the best cat."

Everything was perfect, until one day Murray began to urinate around the house. At first Breanne thought it was simply a behavioral problem, but it didn't take long to realize that he wasn't just misbehaving; he couldn't control his bladder. Breanne took him to a local veterinarian who told her that because of his severe birth defect (no tail), Murray would have chronic problems his entire life and that nothing could be done for him. He further suggested that he should be put to sleep. Breanne had taken him in for a problem she thought was small and fixable. It was unthinkable to her to even consider what she was being told. Murray was just a little over a year old and otherwise healthy. Indignant and somewhat angry, she bundled Murray up and took him home.

Breanne told her mom what the veterinarian had said, and the two of them immediately starting looking through the yellow pages for a second opinion. They found my ad for the Complete Cat Clinic. Maybe it was because his being "incomplete" caused Murray's problem, or maybe it was because I had a cat-only practice, but they chose my office. They made an appointment for the very next day, and on March 23, 2005, I had the pleasure of meeting the toughest pair in town, Breanne and Murray.

With his typical tabby markings, Murray was your average-looking gray alley cat, except for his rear end. He had absolutely no tail. I had to admit that I too liked his softly rounded derriere. He held it higher than the rest of him, showing us how proud he was of what he lacked. There is a breed of cat called a Manx who are bred purposely to have no tails. They come in three varieties: a tailie, which has about two inches of tail; a stumpie, which has about an inch of tail; and a rumpie, which has no tail at all. Murray was a naturally occurring rumpie. The tail is needed, however, because there are nerves that emerge from this lower part of the tail that innervate the bladder and the lower part of the intestine and the rectum. Rumpies often lack these particular nerves resulting in urinary incontinence and lack of bowel control. Even worse, this condition can progress to an inability to urinate or defecate completely.

On the other hand, there was nothing typical about Breanne. She strode in with wild auburn hair and dark fiery eyes. She had tattoos on the back of her neck, her foot, and her ankle. Every finger wore a ring, which led to her long elegantly polished black nails. All in all, she looked like a force to be reckoned with.

Breanne, in her own indomitable way, let me know from the start that she would do anything and everything for Murray. He was a significant part of her life, and in every way, a member of her family. Simply, she loved him. She told me what the other veterinarian had to say. I could read the steadfast determination in her face, and I could see the unconditional love she felt for him. I would not let them down.

I then turned to Murray and gave him a thorough physical examination. He appeared to be in excellent health, and, at that point, his only problem was the incontinence. I prescribed a medication that would help him to control his bladder. Murray would have lifelong problems, I explained, but I felt strongly that together, we could face them one by one and hopefully give Murray a long and healthy life. This time, when Breanne bundled him up to take home, she knew she had found an ally. Through tears of relief, she cracked a smile.

I didn't hear from Breanne for several months, but the next time she called, it was for a much more serious problem. Murray had become severely constipated. He wasn't eating well and wasn't his energetic self. When cats become constipated, they often stop eating and become lethargic, and this was all happening to Murray. I had her put him on a high-fiber diet, and for several months, that was all he needed. When that no longer worked, we added stool softeners. Ultimately, he had to take a medication that helps propel food through the intestinal tract.

Over the next year, Murray was a regular at the clinic. When he wasn't coming in for an enema (You can imagine how much he loved that!), he was coming in because he had been in a fight with another cat and needed stitches. He loved to go outside, and although the outside world can be a dangerous place for a cat, Breanne could not deny Murray anything that made him happy. He was always getting into trouble of one sort or another. One time, he almost lost an eye. He came in with his eye halfway out of its socket. We managed to save the eye, but I believe he couldn't see well out of it ever again. Cat fights, near misses with cars, Murray was always on the edge of disaster. If any cat on this earth had nine lives, I thought, it was Murray.

A year after I met him, in March of 2006, Murray's lower intestine had become so inert that he could no longer have bowel movements. The change of diet, the medication, the stool softeners were no longer helping him. He needed surgery. On March 20, 2006, almost a year to the day that we met, I did a subtotal colectomy on Murray. I removed most of his colon so that his stool would go directly from the small intestine to his rectum and therefore to the outside world.

The surgery was a success, and Murray was able to have bowel movements—lots and lots of bowel movements. He went everywhere and anywhere. I had warned Breanne that this was a possible side effect of the surgery. She said she didn't care. She reminded me of what she had told me right from the start: She would do anything and everything for Murray. She would put up with any inconvenience to herself for him. Is this not true love? I asked myself.

Over the next two years, I continued to treat Murray. I promised Breanne we would deal with his problems as they arose, and we did. He was a regular at the clinic, coming in at least every other week for one thing or another. As his veterinarian, I saw Murray at his worst. I didn't get to see the Murray that ate at the table with them or the Murray that body-bumped the hamster. I saw the Murray that soiled himself on his way over to see me, or the Murray that was recovering from yet another bladder infection. I often wondered if it was fair to put him through all this. But then Breanne would remind me of the wonderful life Murray had at home. He may have a hard life, she said, but he had a good one. He was loved beyond words. He had the best possible care, the best food money could buy, and he had Breanne who dealt with issues that almost no one else I know would put up with. Breanne told me she loved everything about him, even his smelly bottom.

Everyone began to think that he would live forever. He had overcome so many hurdles, fought so many medical battles, and always came back that we all thought he would not just have nine lives but ninety. But that didn't happen.

On Mother's Day 2008, Murray was not able to urinate and quickly became very ill. He didn't eat his usual breakfast and was barely able to move. Breanne rushed him to the local emergency clinic. After extensive testing, Murray was diagnosed with a complete blockage of his urinary tract. He was in critical condition. His only hope was emergency surgery to see if his urinary tract could be repaired to allow him to urinate. Not only that. The operation was going to cost thousands of dollars, which Breanne did not have. Breanne called me to ask my opinion. Since he was too critical to be moved, transporting him to my office was not an option. I had always been there for them and always found a way to help. I wanted to fix Murray once again; after all, wasn't that what I had signed on to do? All I could do was talk to the emergency vet on call and try to advise Breanne over the phone. They told me what they had already told Breanne, that it would be best to put Murray to sleep. They didn't feel he could be saved.

Breanne couldn't and wouldn't let go. Her fierce devotion to Murray and her determination to save him had convinced the doctors to waive their operating fees, thereby saving Breanne thousands of dollars and making the operation, which they still advised against, possible. She told the doctors to go ahead with the surgery. This required creating a new way for the urine to exit his body. They had to take his urethra and redirect it through his abdomen. He would be left with a tube that would have to be drained several times a day.

Murray had emergency surgery that night, but he was still in critical condition the next morning. Breanne called to tell me that Murray had made it through the surgery, but she was having second thoughts about her decision to put him through this. She was asking herself questions that she had not allowed herself to think about before. Had she done the right thing? What kind of life would Murray have after the surgery? But she had promised to do anything and everything she could. How could she give up now? How could she fail him?

Breanne realized that Murray would never be able to go outside again, never be able to get into all the mischief that made his life an adventure. The life she had so intensely fought for would be gone. In a quiet moment, she was able to listen to her heart, and she understood that this was going to be her greatest act of love for Murray.

On May 12, 2008, she let him go.

Murray

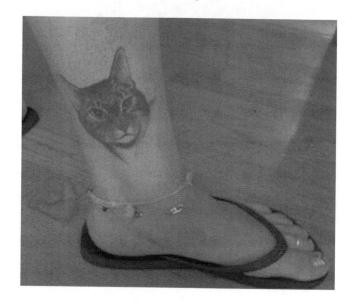

Breanne has a new tattoo

Cats Have Nine Lives

Many people believe that cats have nine lives, but where did this notion come from? Some people think it dates back to ancient Egypt and the cat goddess Bastet who was believed to be immortal. Others believe it stems from cats' uncanny ability to fall from very high places and survive. To many, it looks like they are literally rising from the dead.

The truth is that cats do not really have nine lives. Their ability to land on their feet and cushion a fall is explained by physics. It is a combination of their sense of balance, their relatively light body mass, and the velocity of travel.

We like to believe they have nine lives because as cat lovers, we want them around forever.

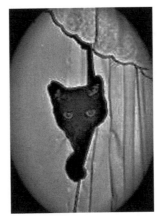

Diane and the Queen of Sheba

Breeding cats has its ups and downs. From the elation of a healthy birthing to the heartache of a stillborn, it can be as exciting and as scary as a roller-coaster ride. Some of them come out easily, head first; others show their feet first, coming out breech. Either way, to watch the miracle of birth take place is one of the highlights of breeding cats. I hold my breath with each contraction. I cheer the mama on, "Just one more contraction and the kitten will be out."

I never get tired of watching this take place—to hear that first meow, to watch them move around frantically, searching blindly for a nipple, then finding it. I am mesmerized as I watch them latch on, move their tiny newborn paws push in and out, in and out, tasting the first milk, the colostrum; and they become calm. And I become calm too.

Day by day, we watch them grow, and we weigh them daily to make sure they are all gaining. They go from what I call the mouse phase to the hamster phase and finally, at about ten days, to being a kitten. Then the fun begins. Every day they become more kittenlike. Taking those first tentative steps, venturing farther away from Mama, their individual personalities begin to emerge. There is the shy one who looks at you but is too afraid to come forward, the alpha kitten who is always the first to do everything, the mama's boy who can't leave his mama's side. We get to know them as individual kittens, not just as a litter. We pick our favorites, give them names, and fall in love.

So it is always bittersweet when they grow old enough to leave the nest and leave us as well. New owners arrive to take their precious bundle home with them. Sometimes we put them on planes, and they fly off to faraway places, to people we have met over the

Internet. We have flown kittens as far away as California, Canada, and Kentucky. We even had someone fly to us from Ohio to get her kitten. The kittens have brought so much to our lives, fun, excitement, and new friends from all across the country. But I never dreamed that one of these kittens would bring my husband and me to Paris, France.

In mid-August 2007, I opened my e-mail to find a most interesting kitten inquiry from a fifteen-year-old girl in Paris.

Dear Madam,

We have been looking for a little baby British shorthair for a very long time, and therefore visited your beautiful website and saw the adorable photos of your kitties—we just fell in love with them. Unfortunately, we live in France; in Paris . . . We were wondering if you occasionally go to Paris and if you do ship worldwide. If so, what are your conditions to that, in euros please?

I do insist on the fact that we are highly interested in your kitten and ready to book one if the delivery doesn't cause any problem . . . We especially fell in love with the little black and white boy (the 35th photo on your "kitten pictures") and we would be very pleased to know if, by any chance, he is available. If not, we would like to know a bit more about the future litters and the colors you expect.

We have been looking for a little black and white harlequin boy for so long, we sincerely hope this time is the right one! Congratulations for your beautiful cattery, we would be very pleased to share with you your pride for the lovely cats you have.

Thank you very much for your help; we are looking forward to hearing from you soon.

Sincerely, Diane

My husband, Peter, loves France; in fact, he lived there for two years as a small child with his mother, a French professor. Since he is fluent in French, I asked him if he would communicate with this family that had inquired about a kitten.

"Maybe they will want us to bring the kitten to them," I teased. "And besides, you can practice your French."

He agreed to take over the exchange with my guidance. For the next two months, e-mails flew through cyberspace, and a kitten was settled on, an adorable chocolate-and-white girl. The only question left was how to get the kitten to Paris.

The chosen kitten

We could fly the kitten over in cargo, but she would have to go unaccompanied. They could fly over to the U.S. and get her. Or Peter and I could make a trip of it and bring her over on board with us. There was a trust that was developing through our correspondence. With each e-mail, I felt we were getting to know them, and they us. They were entrusting me to ensure a healthy kitten; I was trusting that they would provide a good home for one of my babies. Several more e-mails later, Diane and her parents were getting us tickets to Paris. They had decided it was best for the kitten, and I couldn't have agreed more.

"Peter," I said, no longer teasing, "pack your bags."

A date was finally settled on—October 26, 2007. It was the beginning of the school break, and Diane would have two weeks to stay home and bond with her new kitten. There were special arrangements to be made, of course. The kitten had to be microchipped with a particular type of chip. An international health certificate signed by a certified federal veterinarian was also necessary. She had to be at least twelve weeks old and be vaccinated for rabies and distemper. Next, I purchased the perfect carrier for travel. She had to go in style; after all, we were going to Paris. Everyone was envious of this exciting adventure we were about to embark upon, but no one more than Linda, my partner in the breeding program. Although she understood why I was going, she wished that she could go too.

"It doesn't seem fair," she said. "Why do you get to go?"

"Don't worry," I promised, "you'll get to take a kitten on the next trip."

Meanwhile, e-mails continued to arrive from Paris. We were getting closer and closer to departure date, and everyone was getting very excited.

Dear Sharon,

Oh my God, such a precious little baby. Really, she seems to be the kindest cat ever!! I can't believe how lucky I am!!! She is waiting for us!!! We will never thank you enough.

As D-day is coming, I become more and more excited, I am talking and talking but really I can't wait!!! Such a cute little traveler, I hope everything will be fine during the flight; we will be there at the airport, waiting for you of course!!!

4 days!!! Less than 95 hours :-)

Can't wait to meet you three!!! Such a fantastic story.

Hugs,
Diane

October 26 turned out to be a perfect day for travel. The weather was mild, without a cloud in the sky. We'd all waited months for this day to arrive, and no one more than Diane. Her kitten was finally on her way. The plane trip was wonderful. Our little traveler delighted everyone at the airport, popping her head out so see what was going on, purring at just the right moments. She slept most of the way over, something Peter and I were most jealous of.

En route

As the plane landed, all I could think about was Diane's reaction to seeing her kitten for the first time. She had only seen pictures of her, but here we were in person—in the fur, so to speak. We walked off the plane and waited on what seemed like an eternal line to get through customs. Finally through, I could see Diane and her parents as we walked down the ramp. Diane looked up, and there we were. It was a magical moment. The kitten once again popped her head out and gave Diane a welcoming purr. Diane, in turn, gave her kitten a huge kiss. I handed the carrier over to Diane; the kitten was all hers from that moment on.

Diane and her new kitten

Peter and I spent four incredible days in Paris. We went up the Eiffel Tower, ate French croissants, went to the Arc de Triomphe, ate more croissants, walked along the left bank, and again more croissants. In between sightseeing, we visited our new French friends every day, sharing meals and conversation in their typical Parisian apartment. Diane was getting to know her kitten, and we were getting to know each other. Peter practiced his French, and Diane practiced her English. I continued to eat croissants. We have made lifelong friends and will always be welcome to stay with them should we return to Paris.

The day before we left, a name had finally been chosen; she would no longer be known as the kitten. Her official name would be Queen of Saba (Queen of Sheba), and they would call her Saba. The name fit her perfectly, I thought. What a wonderful and unusual journey we had all been on together. From our first e-mail contact, to our arrival in Paris, to our good-byes at the airport, it couldn't have been more exciting or more fun. We had to trust each other all along the way, and that trust made all this possible.

Peter and I returned home with stories to tell and pictures to show. We hear from Diane often as she sends pictures of Saba growing from being a princess to a queen. As hard as it is to part with the kittens, parting with Saba was as easy as eating a French croissant.

Life returned to normal, as it always does. The trip to Paris became a memory all too quickly. Then one day, I opened my e-mail to find an inquiry from a foreign country again. I had promised Linda that the next adventure would be hers to have.

"Linda," I said, "pack your bags. It's your turn to go."

"Where am I going?" she asked.

"Uzbekistan."

Famous Cat-loving Authors

T. S. Elliot, the Nobel Prize-winning British poet and playwright, wrote an entire book of poems about cats entitled *Old Possum's Book of Practical Cats,* which was the basis for the long-running musical *Cats.*

Charles Dickens was also a lover of cats. His first cat, Willamena, produced a litter of kittens in his study. He didn't want to keep them, but he fell in love with one little female kitten that became known as the Master's Cat. She was known to keep him company while he wrote and would even snuff out his reading candle to get his attention.

Edgar Allan Poe was yet another famous author who adored cats. Although many of his stories symbolized cats as sinister, he didn't really see them that way in his everyday life. His tortoiseshell feline, Catarina, was his inspiration behind the story "The Black Cat." Catarina devotedly stayed in bed with Poe's wife as she lay dying of tuberculosis.

Patrick Returns

While Patrick stands on a street corner in Seattle, Washington, I am standing in my office in Brookfield, Connecticut, examining a very sick cat. We are on opposite sides of the country doing what we each want and need to do, taking care of our feline friends. Through cyberspace, Patrick and I continue to get to know one another, as we continue to share our stories that led us to this place.

Anyway, to continue where I left off last time:

My entire childhood was filled with dramatic images of cats: the pink purple crazy Cheshire Cat from Disney's Alice, movies like the moody and surreal 'Curse of the Cat People', Wonder Woman battling the Magic Sphinx, saber-toothed tigers in schoolbooks, etc. One autumn (I think I was ten years old) when I returned to my parent's home in the suburbs after spending a summer at the farm with cats, I decided I would show the neighbor kids my newfound skills with cat communication by staging a little "circus". I taught 4 cats to sit still on top of dairy crates and one cat could jump through a hoop. I drew a decorative poster and printed copies on a Xerox, was thrilled when about 10 neighbor kids showed up to watch. A gang of bullies (one of whom unfortunately was my older brother) ran their bicycles through the crates, yelling and scattering cats in all directions. I was just way too oversensitive back then & cried & cried. I didn't stage another public performance of cat communication for another 35 years! Really too bad I was so oversensitive as a child as I wish to heck now that I'd always been "the cat man," instead I just carried it in the back of my mind until I was 45 years old, then started socializing cats in public again, weird huh? However, I always kept the company of cats and painted lots of pictures of cats my whole life and even the paintings I did of subjects other than cats usually had a cat in there somewhere like in the background. It's like I was always the Pike Place Catman but didn't know it yet.

I was lucky to hit my teenage years right in the middle of the '60s, as that was a unique and wildly creative era of human history.

Kerouac's books got me started hitchhiking all over North America for 10 years, gravitating toward extremely remote areas where other people I knew had also gone to live. The most amount of time I spent was on Stuart Island in the San Juan Islands here in Washington, where I spent 6 years. Stuart Island has no electricity or phones or ferry service and the roads are for horses, not cars. The San Juans are famous for the bald eagles but especially the orca whales, which were around a lot. We survived from my artwork and living off the land, vegetable gardens, clams, codfish, salmon, etc.

Our closest friend was a Chippewa Indian named Little Wolf, who was in his 70s and was an island legend because he claimed to have been discovered as an infant being raised by wolves. (After Little Wolf passed away, I traced down his birth certificate, he'd actually been raised in an orphanage in Minnesota and his real name was Wayne). Anyway what this has to do with cats is that people in remote regions generally have dogs or cats or both for added companionship & even to keep them warm at night. So my living in really remote places was also synonymous with bonding with cats and once again observing a lot of borderline wildcat behavior, for instance my cat frequently chasing down rabbits, chewing off their heads, then playing with the head & so on.

Similar to when my grandfather was drowning cats, we had a very unusual experience on Stuart Island that was a factor in how I eventually became a protector of cats. About a quarter mile to the southeast of Stuart Island is Spieden Island. One side of Speiden Island is trees, the other side, the side seen from my cabin, is a steep slope of all grass, no trees, half a mile long, like an African savanna or so thought the guys who turned Speiden Island into "Safari Island" for three years. They would fly rich gun nuts into the island, where they could shoot and kill exotic animals like antelope, and, for big money, mountain lions and even leopards. This was back in the early 70s; it may not even be legal anymore. So we used to watch the zoo and goings-on with a telescope, there was lots of gunfire, most of it in places we couldn't see, but we saw lots of antelope get killed and over the three years I witnessed the shootings of three mountain lions. The antelopes roamed free and got shot, but the big cats were brought in cages out to the middle of the open plain, were let out of the cages and shot only a short distance from the cage, it was pretty sickening. So similar to when my grandfather used to drown cats, this made some sort of mental impression on me that I later became a sort of protector of cats, and my present day hobby of finding homes for unwanted cats. I returned Seattle in 1980 and have been here ever since.

I, too, traveled to far-off places in the 1970s. One of my more exciting and difficult adventures was a three-month bicycle trip around Europe. We began in Belgium, with the intention of making it to the Rock of Gibraltar. Our trip took us through England, Denmark, Germany, Switzerland, and France as we headed toward Spain and our final destination. As we were traveling through the south of France, we stopped to rest along a riverbank and have a picnic lunch. I heard these little meows and went to look where the sound was coming from. I looked all around and finally realized that the meows were coming from a plastic bag that had been tossed in the river. Like Patrick who, in his early childhood, knew of the act of drowning kittens on the farm, I too had witnessed this awful act on a farm in southern France. It made me sick, and I sat by the side of the river and cried and cried. I could no longer travel through France. I took my bicycle and bought a train ticket to Barcelona, Spain. From there, with a sadness that I never quite shook off, I went home. It took me a long time to "forgive" all of France for this act of cruelty. I never forgot the helpless feeling I had that day, and I know that I was profoundly influenced by it.

I never had a Little Wolf in my life, but I had my share of people that influenced me. One of those people was my anatomy teacher, Professor Pitti, in veterinary school. He was also a breeder of Persian cats. One day, I went to his home where he kept all his cats. He had built a beautiful outdoor area for them where they could chase bugs and laze in the sun. If I were a cat, that's where I would want to live, I thought. It was here that I got my very first cat, Chica. I picked her out among the kittens romping around in the yard. I was fortunate enough to enjoy her wonderful company for the next sixteen and a half years. My professor not only taught me anatomy, but he set a standard of care for his cats that I continue to try to live up to, and I will forever be thankful for that.

Patrick in the 1970s with a feline friend

Cats in Nursery Rhymes

Most of us grew up with nursery rhymes; they are a part of American culture. Most of them didn't really make too much sense or were hard to figure out, but we didn't care. As children, we listened to them again and again and again. With such classics as "Pussycat, pussycat, where have you been?"; "Hey diddle diddle, the cat and the fiddle"; "The Owl and the Pussycat"; "Two Little Kittens"; "Three Little Kittens"; "A Cat Came Fiddling Out of a Barn"; and so many others. It's no wonder that so many of us grew up to have such a fondness to the beautiful feline. Whether we had one as a pet or not, they were still an important part of our childhood through these wonderful nursery rhymes.

Dr. Sharon Eisen, Chica, and Bentley

When I was a little girl, I wasn't a cat person. In fact, I was completely obsessed with dogs. My *World Book Encyclopedia* had the dog section dog-eared, and I could name every breed of dog by the age of seven. So it was quite surprising to me that when I became a veterinarian and started my own practice, I decided to open a cat-only hospital. How did a devotee of dogs become infatuated with cats?

I never understood cats, never really knew what they were like. I dissected a cat in anatomy class, literally held a cat's heart in my hand. I knew what parasites made them their hosts or what diseases they were likely to get. I learned breeds of cats, life expectancy, gestation periods, and kitten mortality. I learned how to neuter a cat and fix a dislocated hip. But I had never lived with a cat.

During my last year of veterinary school, I got my first cat. She was a blue cream Persian whom I named Chica. I was coming down the homestretch in veterinary school, on my way to achieving that hard-earned degree; my dog was staying with my parents, and I was lonely for animal companionship. They say you don't really know someone until you live with them. I learned about cats when Chica came to live with me, and it started my long, enduring love affair with cats.

Chica was the most enchanting creature to me. She had the softest, most luxurious fur I had ever run my fingers through. I could spend hours just looking at her, gracefully leaping onto a dresser seven feet up in the air, balancing herself along something scarily narrow, slowly licking her fur over and over until she was satisfied with its shine and cleanliness. She had some of the most endearing qualities too. Each morning, she would wake me by sucking on my earlobes, a habit she would continue to have in old age, sucking on any earlobe she found available. When I brought her to the clinic, she would often sneak up behind someone who was sitting in the waiting room and grab his or her earlobe. It tickled and usually made people laugh. Unlike a dog, she didn't wait anxiously at the door for me when I came home. Rather, I would find her curled up in my favorite chair, warming it up for me (I was giving her the benefit of the doubt). She shared so much of my life, my marriage, the birth of my daughter, a bitter divorce, and the opening of the cat hospital.

Chica lived to a respectable old age of seventeen, ultimately dying of kidney failure, the most common cause of death in the older cat. She was "puppy" love, my first cat, and because of that she will always hold a very special place in my heart.

Chica

Everyone who has loved cats has one or maybe two that stand out above the rest. Something about them makes you love them the most. Maybe it was a special-needs kitty or a kitty that was there during a difficult time in your life. My special cat was Bentley, a lilac British Shorthair. Everyone thinks his or her kitten is the most beautiful, but Bentley really was the most beautiful kitten, at least in the cat show world. He became an international winning cat, winning Best in Show several times. He was a Supreme Grand

Champion and set the standard of the breed for years to follow. Because of his lilac color, people used to call him the purple kitty. He had a fans club, cheering him on at the shows. Judges wanted to steal him; spectators wanted to buy him. His manners equaled his looks, and he went on to be in television commercials and print ads. He even made an appearance on Animal Planet, a very popular channel devoted to animals. He was a cat that didn't have a hiss in his vocabulary. He was magic. He had looks, poise, talent, and popularity. And he was mine.

I had a waiting list of people who wanted his kittens. Everyone was waiting in anticipation of what he would produce. But that was not to happen. Bentley wouldn't breed, and ultimately, I neutered him with the hopes of showing him again in the alter class. One week after his surgery, Bentley went into congestive heart failure. I came in to the office to find him unable to get any air into his lungs, his mouth open, gasping for air. The veterinarian in me completely shut down. I couldn't see through my tears. My sense of helplessness was profound. I scooped him up and brought him to a veterinarian in town whom I knew and trusted. He spent three long days there and, thankfully, made it through the crisis. He was diagnosed with hypertrophic cardiomyopathy, a type of heart disease that causes the muscles of the heart to thicken, narrowing the heart chambers and rendering the heart ineffective at pumping blood. His heart was so weak that it was a miracle he survived. My dear, lovely Bentley, the cat with a heart of gold, had heart disease. We put him on medication to help his heart function and keep him out of heart failure. He responded well to the medication and flourished for years. He was even able to do a few more gigs, something he really enjoyed. He had an opportunity to be in a commercial for a major credit card company, and hoping to convince the company that Bentley was the cat for them, we decided to photograph him sitting on a Rolls-Royce. One of my clients owned a Rolls and was more than happy to lend his car for the shoot. In fact, he polished her up before driving over to the clinic. On a fabulous sunny day, we all went outside to place Bentley atop a shiny silver Rolls-Royce. He didn't get the shoot, but that photograph remains one of our favorites to this day.

Five and a half wonderful years flew by. Bentley was the king and the ambassador of the clinic. He would perch himself up on the front desk. He had the ability to sit so eerily still that people coming in thought he was a statue. He startled many a client when he finally moved, stretching himself out, repositioning himself to lie back down. He would look at you with his deep golden eyes, and you would simply melt. If he wasn't sitting on the front desk, people would ask where he was. Clients felt cheated if they didn't see Bentley before they left. He became the clinic fixture, and everyone knew him and loved him.

Where Chica was young love, Bentley was a more mature love. I held on to him the tightest when I battled cancer in January 2000. We were both going to be survivors. Then one day, without warning, he got sick again. He wasn't interested in food anymore, his energy level declined, and he became withdrawn. That same sense of helplessness overcame me; I felt desperate to help him. I tried different medications, different foods, new tests, anything I could think of. I consulted with colleagues, called specialists in the field of cardiology; I was ready to do anything to save him. It was next to impossible for me to focus on anything other than saving my beloved Bentley. But I couldn't make him better.

One week later, Bentley drifted off to sleep and never woke up. So often, as pet owners, we are forced to make the most difficult of all decisions—when to euthanize a beloved pet. When does it become the right thing to do? How do we know when the time is right? I didn't have to make that decision with Bentley. It was yet another gift he gave to me.

Nonetheless, I was inconsolable. I was angry. With all my veterinary knowledge, with all my years of experience, how could I not have helped him? I learned a lot about grief in the weeks to follow. I spent hours in my office, going over the "should haves" and "could haves." I felt guilty about everything and anything. And then the strangest thing happened. I heard a little repetitive sound at my office window and looked up to find a brightly colored goldfinch pecking at the glass. I walked up to the window and watched him for a few moments until he flew away. Every day, for a week, that same goldfinch came to the same window at the same time of day. I'm not a superstitious person, but I became convinced that this bird was trying to tell me something. Could this be a message from Bentley? What was the little birdie trying to tell me?

It wasn't something I could put into words right away. It was a feeling, not a thought. I began to smile. The bird never came back after that. I had gotten the message. Bentley was all right, and I needed to be too. I had a cat hospital to run and cats to take care of. Looking back, my love affair with cats developed slowly and steadily. From Chica, who was my earlobe-sucking alarm clock, to Bentley, my shining star, this die-hard devotee of dogs had turned into a cat-loving, cat-fancying addict. Although I grew up without cats and didn't have one until I was an adult, it feels like they have always been a part of my life. Now, I can't imagine living without one or two or ten.

Bentley on the Rolls-Royce

Morris

Finicky and egotistical, Morris was a star, appearing in a series of television cat food commercials with a large and loyal fan following. Bob Martwick, a professional animal trainer, rescued the original Morris, a fourteen-pound orange tabby from a Chicago animal shelter.

Although the same cat didn't always play him, over the years, Morris became part of our lives. All cats that played Morris have been rescued either coming from an animal shelter or cat rescue. The 9Lives Cat Food wasn't his only gig. He became honorary director of Star-Kist Foods with veto power of any cat food flavor that he did not like. Even President Nixon was a fan, inviting Morris to cosign the National Animal Protection Bill with his paw print.

In 1983, *Time* magazine declared Morris "the feline Burt Reynolds." He has received many awards including the PATSY Award (the Picture Animal Top Star of the Year Award) from the American Humane Association and the Cats' Meow Award given by New York Animal Medical Center in 1992.

Morris's philosophy in life: "The cat who doesn't act finicky soon loses control of his owner."

The Bereavement Group

The pet bereavement group started shortly after my beloved Bentley died. I'd always felt that a support group was needed for those of us who were suffering the loss of a pet, but it was Bentley's passing and my own intense grief that was the impetus to get it going.

The *Handbook of Psychiatry* defines grief as "the normal response to the loss of a loved one by death." When we lose a beloved person in our lives, grief is expected and normal. There are places to go and people to talk to that will help us cope with those feelings. But when a pet dies and you grieve, you'll often hear things like "Get over it, it's just a pet," or "What's the matter with you, are you nuts?" Even at the office, where we understand how passionate our clients feel toward their pets, people are embarrassed to cry and show their emotion. With an understanding hug, we tell them that the clinic is the one place that they can cry, and we will not pass judgment; in fact, we will completely understand what they are feeling.

On June 11, 2005, Bentley died. He left a void not just in me, but also at the clinic where he was king. Everyone who had ever set foot in the clinic loved Bentley, and I knew that they would want to be made aware of his passing. Since pets don't get written up in the obituaries (although perhaps they should), I decided to write an article for the local newspaper eulogizing Bentley. At the same time, I announced that I would be starting a pet support/ bereavement group in his honor. I left my phone number and e-mail address for people to contact me.

The response was overwhelming. Cards came flooding in from so many of my friends and clients expressing their sympathy. E-mails arrived too, full of stories of other people's grief and the struggles they were having coping with their sadness and loss. There was no place to turn, no one to talk to. Many expressed their gratitude that a support group for pet bereavement was being started; they not only wanted to come to it, but also needed to.

I had been in a support group during my battle with cancer, but I had no idea how to facilitate one. I called Lynn, the group leader of my group, who I had become close to, and asked her if she would run the first few meetings to help me get started. She didn't have to think long before saying yes.

"Grief is grief and loss is loss," Lynn told me. "The feelings are the same, no matter what the cause. I would be happy to help. I have had my share of sadness over the loss of my cat too. I understand."

I studied grief; there was a lot to learn, and I wanted to be as prepared as possible. Kübler-Ross wrote on the subject in her landmark book, *On Death and Dying*. She describes five stages of grief: (1) denial, (2) anger, (3) bargaining, (4) depression, and (5) acceptance. She also states that they may not always occur in this order and that not everyone will go through all the stages, but everyone will experience at least two. Another way of looking at grief is described by Dr. Roberta Temes in her book *Living with an Empty Chair: A Guide through Grief.* She describes three stages of grief: (1) numbness—mechanical functioning, social isolation; (2) disorganization—intensely painful feelings of loss; and (3) reorganization—reentry into a more "normal" social life.

Together with Lynn, I was ready to begin the group. We began meeting on Thursday evenings at the cat clinic. There is always a cat or two roaming around the office, and I thought it would be good therapy to have a cat jump on a lap or purr during the meetings. At our first meeting, we had about ten people. We sat in a circle, introduced ourselves, and shared why we were there. It was deeply moving and reassuring to discover that we weren't crazy after all and that many people felt the same way. We were all experiencing profound grief over the loss of a beloved pet. Someone confessed that they hadn't grieved this much when her father passed away.

Another shared that she was having difficulty going back to work because her sadness was so pervasive. Yet another said her husband was worried about her mental health. One young woman said her cat was her "child," and she was overwhelmed with grief, unable to function.

The meeting gave everyone an opportunity to talk about the cat that they had loved and lost. We listened carefully, asking more specific questions about their cat: "What color was he?"; "What were his favorite things to do?"; "What was your relationship like?"; "What did he/she mean to you?" Talking helped enormously. It was therapeutic to be able to describe your cat and what the relationship meant to you and know that you would not be judged. We were there to understand and to help. We let people cry; in fact, crying was encouraged.

The meeting lasted one hour, and Lynn told me in advance that it was important to end on time. We ended in a support circle, held hands, and Lynn left us with some parting words of encouragement. Everyone left feeling more validated than when they arrived.

Something good was coming out of Bentley's passing. I knew I was doing something meaningful and worthwhile. The following week, we had the same ten people and a couple new ones join the group. Again, we went around introducing ourselves and explaining what brought us to the group. Some of my own clients were there, expressing their sorrow over cats that I had been asked to put to sleep. Ellen was there, someone I never expected to join the group. She had such a hard exterior; I thought she could handle anything. But there she was, showing us her soft interior, bruised and in pain. There was Jen who came with her fiancé, trying to deal with the loss of her precious cat Destiny, who had been with her through her toughest and most challenging times. There was Christine Frost who had just lost Sydney, a cat she called her best friend.

Over the next several months, we continued to meet at the clinic on Thursday evenings. Some people felt better enough and stopped coming after two to four meetings; others needed a lot more time and support. One time, we had everyone bring pictures of their cats to show everyone—sort of like show-and-tell in elementary school. We passed around the pictures, admiring these very loved and missed felines. It was a time to honor their special cats and to show respect for their relationship. Sharing the pictures was particularly helpful in the healing process. I always knew things were going well when laughter could be heard in the room. I knew healing was taking place. We were collectively working through the stages of grief; however, I would add a stage of grief to the list: guilt. Everyone felt guilt about something. Did they put their cat down too soon? Did they wait too long and let their cat suffer? Could they have saved their cat if they had done more medically? Did they not see something that they should have seen? The list of guilt-ridden questions goes on and on, and everyone felt it. We helped each person through those guilt feelings by analyzing them one by one and dispelling any false ideas.

Our ultimate goal, of course, was to reach acceptance and then reorganization so that we could move on and hopefully bring another kitty into our lives and love them just as much. They would never replace Destiny or Sidney or Bentley, but they would fill that void left by their being physically gone. We missed them so very, very much.

The bereavement group is a chapter of the cat clinic that I am very proud of. Bentley would be proud too.

News-Times Archives

THIS STORY HAS BEEN FORMATTED FOR EASY PRINTING

The article you requested is displayed below.

Mourning Fido and Fluffy

Author(s): Kamilla Gary THE NEWS-TIMES
Date: June 20, 2005
Section: Local
Article ID: story72297

BROOKFIELD—Looking at a movie of her beloved cat, Bentley, Dr. Sharon Eisen doesn't try to hold back tears. "Look how handsome he is," Eisen said.

Eisen, a veterinarian who has run the Complete Cat Veterinary Clinic in Brookfield for the past 14 years said goodbye to Bentley, a lilac British short hair, on June 11. Bentley was diagnosed with cardiomyopathy, a congenital heart defect shortly after his second birthday.

Eisen stabilized his condition with medication, but he died at 7.

"We're really, really missing him and grieving him," Eisen said. The cat lived at the clinic, serving as a furry greeter.

"When you walked into the clinic, he would be on the counter. He was the office manager and ambassador," said Linda Francese, veterinary technician. Francese recalled coming to the clinic to interview for her job and staying to play with the exotically colored cat with the little lilac-colored nose—as a lot of people did.

Bentley spent his early life as a show cat, becoming the first lilac short hair shown in the United States. He was named a Supreme Grand Champion and International winner.

He was a sweet-tempered cat with an agent, Cathryn Long, owner of All Creatures Great and Small. Bentley appeared in both print and television advertisements. In February, he shot a commercial for the allergy medicine Claritin.

Eisen knows the pain of losing a pet is real and can be a crushing blow to a pet owner.

The doctor wants to create a bereavement group for people caring for a dying pet or those who have experienced a pet's death. She said a group would also help people with trouble deciding whether to have their pets euthanized.

"People feel guilty, people feel loss," Eisen said. "They think 'Could I have done something to prevent the loss.'Y"

Connecticut's only pet bereavement support group is held the second Tuesday of each month at Norwalk Town Hall. It was started 20 years ago by Dr. Richard McFarland of the Norwalk Animal Hospital and M. Patricia Gallagher, a former nun and grief counselor. Gallagher sent letters to every veterinarian in Fairfield County, and McFarland was the only one to respond.

"It occurred to her as she counseled folks there might be a need on the veterinary side," McFarland said. He said meetings tend to ebb and flow with some nights where no one shows up and some nights where many attend.

Gallagher said the loss of a pet, who gives unconditional love, is sometimes harder than losing a human.

She said it's best to seek out people to talk about the loss.

"Grief shared is grief diminished," Gallagher said.

For people who can't talk about the loss of a pet, she suggests they get a notebook and write down their feelings.

"Just try to conclude it with a happy memory," Gallagher said.

Support groups are mostly advertised through word of mouth. McFarland said not many veterinarians refer clients who have lost pets. Gallagher said in the past few months, she has only held one meeting because not many people know about the group—or they don't feel comfortable attending.

Eisen said in some cases, people might grieve for a pet and be made to feel like they're crazy for doing so.

"You need to find people who get it, seek them out," Eisen said.
"There will be those who think you're nuts and will make you feel worse."

Marge Grossman, a licensed clinical social worker who has had a counseling practice in Stamford for 12 years, said she began adding pet bereavement counseling a year ago.

"It's very real and very serious," Grossman said. The losses can be especially difficult for the elderly and shut-ins.

"Maybe people don't think it's legitimate enough to seek help," Grossman said. "People seek help for anxiety and depression, but they don't think they're supposed to seek help when they lose a pet."

Eisen plans a living memorial for Bentley—a lilac bush planted outside her practice where she will scatter some of Bentley's ashes.

Eisen looks forward to helping those coping with the loss of beloved pets.

"The deeper the joy, the greater the pain," Eisen said. "When you give people the opportunity to talk about their pets, it's cathartic to feel they can share."

Cat Proverbs

There are literally hundreds of proverbs that have the cat as the main topic. Here are some fun ones that we scratched up:

"In a cat's eye, all things belong to cats."—English proverb

"Beware of people who dislike cats."—Irish proverb

"After dark all cats are leopards."—Native American proverb

"Happy owner, happy cat. Indifferent owner, reclusive cat."—Chinese proverb

"A cat has nine lives. For three he plays, for three he strays, and for the last three he stays."—English proverb

"Happy is the home with at least one cat."—Italian proverb

"I gave an order to a cat, and the cat gave it to its tail."—Chinese proverb

"A cat may go to a monastery, but she still remains a cat."—Ethiopian proverb

"The cat is nature's beauty."—French proverb

"When the cat is away the mice will play."

"The cat is honest when the meat is out of her reach."

"A cornered cat becomes as fierce as a lion."

Christine Frost and Sydney

They say that a dog is man's best friend, and that may be true for some people, but not for Christine Frost. For her, it was a gray tabby and white cat named Sydney.

"He was my best friend," she said. "I have a special place for all my other cats, but what I had with Sydney, I don't think I'll ever find with another cat."

I asked her what made Sydney so special. What made him her best friend?

It all started when a friend of hers found a cat on her school campus. Christine had just moved away from home in upstate New York, and her friend brought the cat over to her new place thinking she might need a little companionship in her new apartment. Christine took in the boarder, agreeing that a little company might be nice. Sydney was a "girl" that turned out to be a boy, but that's another story. At the time, Christine had no idea how important this cat would become for her.

Christine and Sydney went through many firsts together: her first apartment away from her family; a new, bigger city to get used to; her first real job; her first major boyfriend; and the inevitable first heart-wrenching breakup. At the end of the day, it was Sydney she came home to, always there ready to cuddle up to her and give her a welcoming purr. When Christine would travel to her parents' home in upstate New York, a seven-hour trip, she would take Sydney with her. She would do the driving while Sydney was the copilot. He was the best traveling buddy; he never complained about what music was on the radio, and he never asked, "Are we there yet?" Sydney, who started out as a simple companion to Christine, was turning into an inseparable friend.

Like any friendship, it had its challenges. Sydney, being a teenager, would get into all sorts of mischief. The toy mouse she bought him was disemboweled, leaving green stuffing all over her new beige rug. He tore up her new sofa, climbed the curtains, and broke his share of glassware. But that was the least of it. His coup de grâce was when Christine came home to find her water bed had been turned into a swimming pool. Was Sydney testing her patience and their friendship?

One day, Christine came home and found that her apartment had been burglarized. When she saw the broken window, she understood how they got in and immediately realized that Sydney could have gotten out. She was frantic at the thought that Sydney might have somehow disappeared or gotten hurt in the incident. Where was Sydney? Before looking around the house to see what might have been stolen, her first thought was to find him. She looked out of the broken window and saw him cowering and shaking on the fire escape. She quickly took him in her arms, hugging him like never before. If she were ever angry with him for his antics, she forgave him all. He was a cat, after all, and cats don't like to sleep in water beds that go *swish-swish* in the night. Afterward, she promised she would never get another water bed. She also decided to move to a safer neighborhood, where both she and Sydney could go to bed with peace of mind. With their move to New Milford, Connecticut, a new veterinarian had to be found for Sydney; and as fortune and fate would have it, she found us, the Complete Cat Clinic.

As Sydney settled into young adulthood, so did Christine. They were growing up side by side, learning life's lessons, the good and the bad. Shortly after they settled into the new house, Christine had to face her hardest challenge yet. Her mother, who had a debilitating lung disease, developed pneumonia and passed away at the young age of sixty-three. Christine's father, who had neglected his own health in order to take care of her mother, died of a massive heart attack only a few months later. He was also only sixty-three. Christine lost both of her parents in a span of four months. It was almost more than she could bear. Christine turned to Sydney, burying her tears in his soft gray-and-white fur. She could always find the comfort she needed when she looked at his soulful golden eyes, a solace that only a best friend can give you.

It wasn't long after Christine lost her parents that Sydney became dangerously ill. Now it was Christine's turn to help him. Sydney couldn't urinate, a condition that can lead to death in only forty-eight hours. Stones had formed in his bladder, which had gotten lodged in his narrow urethra. If the condition persists, the urine can go back up into the kidneys and cause kidney failure or the bladder can rupture, causing acute peritonitis and death. She was told to take him to Tufts Veterinary Hospital, where he would have the best and most advanced medical care anywhere in the Northeast. If anyone could save him, they could. Without hesitation, she loaded him into the car and, through tears and fear, drove the four hours to get to Tufts. They had been on many a road trip together, including the long drives to upstate New York, but none had the urgency that this trip had. When she arrived, she said, "Please fix him, do anything, I can't lose him. He is my best friend."

Sydney had emergency surgery that night, a procedure that turned him back to a girl, but that, too, is another story. Christine was given the news and, in two seemingly endless days, went back to Tufts to bring him home.

"The day I brought him home from Tufts was one of the best days of my life," she said, "my best friend was coming home."

Sadly, our cat friends age more quickly and reach old age long before we do. Seven years after Sydney's brush with death, at the ripe old age of nineteen, his body gave out. He, quietly and without fear, went to sleep for the last time.

It was at this time that the Complete Clinic started its bereavement group. Christine felt she had to be a part of it and came to the very first meeting. It would help her get over her own grief, she thought, but more than that, she felt she could help others with their grief. She had been through so much sadness and tragedy in her own life that she had much to share and teach.

Since Sydney's passing, Christine has had other cats in her life. There is Bailey who, oddly enough, had a urinary tract blockage just like Sydney and needed the very same surgery, which he also had done at Tufts. Christine has also become a member of Noah's Wish, an organization that helps animals in disaster situations, such as Hurricane Katrina. She has learned animal CPR and—together with her two nieces, ages 8 and 11—volunteers at a local animal shelter once a week.

Christine believes she will never have another best friend like Sydney, but I am not so sure. When Dr. Eisen and I decided to adopt Mick Dundee, our very special chocolate-and-white British Shorthair stud whom we recently retired, we thought of only one person, Christine. When we offered her Mickie, it took her about one minute to say yes. We both have a feeling that Christine will soon be able to say, "I never thought I would say this, but I have a new best friend, and his name is Mick Dundee."

Sydney

Christine and her best friend, Sydney

Mick Dundee

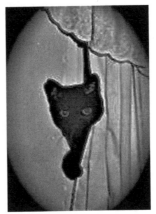

The Japanese Maneki Neko

An old Japanese legend tells of a cat that waved a sword at a Japanese landlord. The landlord, intrigued by the gesture, walked toward the cat. Moments later, a lightning bolt struck where the landlord had been previously standing. The landlord believed his good fortune was due to the cat's fortuitous action. From that time forward, the cat with the waving hand became a symbol of good luck, particularly in business, to draw in money.

In today's modern world, you will often find the Maneki Neko sitting next to a cash register in Asian-owned stores. They are also said to bring good luck in homes, but they must face the front door. When you walk into Linda's house, the Maneki Neko is one of the first things you'll see. In fact, she has seven, in different colors and sizes. Every little bit helps.

Robert, Lauren, and Columbo

They say that black cats bring bad luck, but for Robert and Lauren Ross, nothing could have been farther from the truth. Like Peter Falk's most well-known irascible character, Columbo, a black cat, entered their lives, solved a mystery, and saved a life.

Robert had it all, from a dream job working as a commercial airline pilot to a happy and satisfying marriage to his wife Lauren. His life was in order: a great, well-paying job that he loved, a clean and orderly house, just the way Robert wanted it. Everything had its place, and his life was tidy, neat, and clean. That was when the bottom fell out.

One day, while riding his bicycle, an automobile struck him. His injuries were severe enough to end his dream career as a commercial airline pilot and leave him with chronic, debilitating back pain. It was a devastating and life-altering blow. In order to pay the bills, he took a job on Wall Street, but it was "just" a job. His company merged with another, and he was abruptly laid off. It was literally insult to injury, and Robert began to sink deeper and deeper into a very severe depression. His wife didn't know what to do; therapy wasn't helping, and medication wasn't working. Robert was at the lowest point in his life. He often thought of ending what he felt had become a hopeless and meaningless existence. He felt he had nothing and no one to live for.

It was at this point in his life when, on a hot, humid summer day, a black cat appeared out of nowhere. He just kept hanging around Robert and Lauren's apartment in the complex where they had lived for the past four years. He was dirty, unkempt, and scraggly; and he was homeless. He was everything Robert aspired not to be, but could Robert end up like this cat? He looked at this poor creature, not with sympathy, but with disdain. Robert, who had never wanted any living creature in his home, told his wife not to feed it. If you feed a cat, they'll just keep coming back, and a cat was the last thing Robert wanted or thought he needed in his life. His perfectly ordered world had already been turned upside down. A dirty stray cat would only make his life more miserable, he thought. But like Falk's character Columbo, this cat would not be deterred. Although there were many other apartments he could have gone to, it was at Robert's door that he sat diligently, day after day. Was he using Columbo's line to get in the door? "There's just one thing that bothers me, sir."

He continued to sit by the door for several months. This cat was on the outside meowing to be let in while Robert was inside crying to be let out. One night, the cat's persistence paid off. It was a dark and rainy night, right around Thanksgiving. Robert saw him out there on the stoop, under the overhang, trying to stay out of the rain. It was two o'clock in the morning, and with his flashlight in hand to illuminate the porch, he brought out his computer box and set it up out there for the cat to crawl into. He didn't know it then, but this small gesture was the first step that would lead to his release from the emotional agony that had become his life.

The next morning, when Lauren opened the front door, the cat ran into the house. Robert was lying down on the sofa; to him, it was another day to try and get through, another day of anguish and self-pity.

"Don't let the cat in," he shouted.

At that moment, this very gruff, very clever cat jumped up on the couch, curled himself in Robert's arms, and purred himself to sleep. Robert not only let the cat into the apartment, but he also let him in to his arms and to his heart. It was then, and only then, that his healing could and would begin.

"I fell in love with him at that moment. But it was a different kind of love. It was an unconditional love, like the love a parent feels toward their children," he says.

Lauren called him Columbo, she says, because she enjoys detective stories and he seemed so black and mysterious and scruffy, like the Peter Falk character. I think he came with the name, and it was somehow transmitted to Lauren in cat speak. Everything about this cat was a mystery. Why did he pick their apartment to plant himself in front of? Why did he so readily and easily make himself at home once allowed in the apartment?

"Robert is not the same person I married," Lauren says. "Someone once told me that you don't choose a cat but that a cat chooses you. Well, thank goodness, this cat chose us. Robert may go a little overboard with him, but I'd rather have it this way than see Robert the way he was before."

Going overboard is a bit of an understatement. One day, Robert went to the Sony store and bought two $10,000, sixty-inch plasma televisions for Columbo's viewing pleasure. When they were delivered, he made sure they were angled and installed with the cat's viewing in mind. Columbo's favorite shows are *Two and a Half Men* and the Food Network. If he hears the music to *Two and Half Men*, he will come running from wherever he is in the apartment to watch it.

Robert and Lauren and Columbo have settled into a life together. Columbo wants his food at certain times of the day and has trained Robert to get it for him. They cannot sleep without each other. Columbo knows just how to walk on Robert's back to help with the chronic pain he suffers with. Lauren will sometimes jokingly ask Robert if he has helped Columbo with his homework.

It was misdiagnoses that brought this newly formed family to my office. His local veterinarian had diagnosed Columbo with kidney disease and told him Columbo had three months to a year to live. Robert was beyond crushed. How was it possible that Columbo, who didn't seem sick at all, could be dying? He did seem constipated, but kidney disease?

Robert had been going to see a career counselor in the hopes of finding a new and meaningful path for himself. On his next scheduled visit with her, he couldn't focus on himself because of the news he had just heard about Colombo. He couldn't think about anything else and found himself telling the counselor the entire story of Columbo. The counselor, a long-standing client of mine as well as a good friend, suggested he talk to me about Columbo.

I spoke with Robert several times over the phone. He sent me all of Columbo's medical records along with the lab work that had been done to date. I saw nothing in the lab work or the history that made me believe Columbo had kidney disease. To be sure, I wanted to do my own physical and my own blood work on Columbo. Without hesitation, Robert brought Columbo to my office. After a thorough physical; a long, detailed conversation with Robert; and a careful analysis of the results of the blood work that I had run, I could say without doubt that Columbo was here to stay and hopefully for a very, very long time. No, he did not have kidney disease, of that I was certain. All he needed was a slight change of diet to help him with his constipation.

And this is how I learned of Robert and Columbo's remarkable story, a story of a cat that found a way to help a man recover from a profound depression and change his life forever. Robert no longer sweats the small stuff, like a little dirt on the floor. Columbo has taught him how to live day to day, how to focus less on the future and more on living each moment more fully. Most importantly, Columbo has taught Robert the meaning of unconditional love, something Robert never thought he could understand, let alone feel. It was in the giving and caring to this mysterious black cat that he freed himself from self-pity and allowed him to step outside his depression and leave it on the front stoop.

As they are about to leave my office, I see Columbo turn in my direction. "There's just one more thing that bothers me, Doc," he winks.

Columbo

Lauren and Columbo

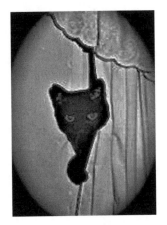

Black Cats and Witches

Black cats and witches go back to the Middle Ages. Some people believed that cats were witches in disguise while others believed that black cats were witches' familiars (beings that aid witches in performing their craft). Some other superstitions include a kitten born in May will be a witch's cat; if a black cat walks into the room of an ill person and the person later dies, it is blamed on the cat; if a cat crosses a person's path without harming him or her, it indicates that the person is protected by the devil. Folklore also has it that if a witch becomes human, a black cat will no longer reside in her home.

Although, in 2009, people no longer believe black cats are witches in disguise, during Halloween, kids still love to dress up as black cats (and witches); and many shelters will not adopt out a black cat during the month of October.

Laurie, Barry, and Demi

Demi was trouble from day one. I never liked him, even as a kitten. When my friend Laurie and her husband, Barry, decided to get a new kitten, I offered to help them pick one out from the North Shore Animal Shelter. Laurie and I were at one end of the room oohing and aahing over a Persian-like kitten that was meowing and looking ever so cute. But Barry had other ideas. His favorite was a little black-and-white kitten hiding and snarling in the corner of one of the many cages filling the shelter. This particular kitten was infested with ear mites and would need weeks of diligent treatment, so I advised Barry that perhaps he should choose one that would require less fussing over. But Barry's mind was made up. He saw something in this kitten, a meeting of the minds perhaps, and would take home no other. As they bundled up their new kitten to bring home, I could have sworn I saw the kitten smirk at me as if to say, "See, even though you advised against me, I'm getting out of here." There was even an unnerving, evil look in his little dark amber eyes.

For the next three months, Barry went through boxes of Q-tips and Kleenex in order to rid Demi of the mites. He fought with him day after day to clean and medicate his ears until they finally looked clean. On my visits to their house, I always checked his ears with my otoscope until the day he was finally free of the mites and no more medication was needed. He challenged me every time I went near him, and more often than not, I left bloodied from a scratch or a bite. I always wondered if it was the constant ear cleanings that made Demi so angry at the world. When I asked Barry why he named him Demi, he tells me it was because he had half a brain. Then Laurie reminds him it was because he was half-black and half-white. I wasn't sure which it really was.

One morning, when Demi was just barely a year of age, he decided he wanted to learn how to fly. Laurie was alarmed when Demi didn't wake as usual, her demanding to be fed. She called his name over and over and looked everywhere for him, checking his usual hangouts. Demi did not appear to be in the apartment. She glanced over to the living room window and noticed that it was open, and the screen was missing. They lived on the sixth floor. She knew right away what that meant. Laurie ran over and looked out the window, down to the alley below. From the sixth floor, she could just make out the screen with Demi underneath it. She was sure he was dead. In her nightgown, she raced out of the apartment, took the elevator down the six flights to the basement, and ran out to the alley. She lifted the screen off him, fully expecting him to be dead. Amazingly, Demi was still alive. Broken and in pain, she lifted him up in her arms and rushed him to a local animal hospital. X-rays revealed that both of his forelegs were badly broken, and his jaw was dislocated. Miraculously, he had no life-threatening damage, and everything could be surgically repaired. The little adoptee now became a bionic $1,000 cat. Both his front legs had to be wired, pinned, and splinted; and his jaw had to be wired together as well. Since he had splints put on both his front legs, he was not able to walk in a forward direction. Demi had to push against the splints and propel himself to move in backward circles. It was quite a laughable sight. He now became what is called a high-rise cat. These are cats that fall from high buildings and sometimes live to tell about it. They sustain particular injuries based on the height of the fall. If Demi had fallen from the fourth or the eighth floor, he might not have lived. But he flew out of precisely the sixth floor and survived. Coincidence? If he wasn't already a cat with attitude, I could have blamed his unpleasantness to the fall and having to endure months of ridicule. But Demi was out to get me from day one; I was sure of it.

One of the things that made Demi so endearing was the way he would attack people's ankles when you visited his home. He was particularly fond of attacking mine, and Barry's best friend, Joel. I would walk into their apartment, and from some unknown corner, Demi would suddenly appear and attach himself to my ankle. If I was sitting on their sofa, I was sure to lift my legs up or Demi would lunge at my feet from underneath the couch. Laurie and Barry always assured me that he was sweet and loving to them although I found it hard to believe. Why did he hate me so? Could it be because I neutered him on my desk? (I didn't have my own practice back then.) Was it because I told Barry not to take him from the shelter? Or was it because I laughed myself silly watching him go round and round for months as he healed from the high-rise incident?

No sooner had Demi healed from almost plunging to his death that his next brush with mortality followed. This time, he decided to swallow several feet of string. His intestinal tract became completely obstructed, and another frantic visit to the emergency hospital was needed. Again, with emergency surgery to remove the string, Demi would live to see another day. Now the mite-infested adoptee became a $2,000 cat. Two thousand dollars is still a large sum of money, but back in the 1980s, it was an almost impossible sum to come up with, especially for a young, growing family.

Visits to see my closest friends were fraught with fear. As much as I loved going to see my dear friends, I found myself dreading the inevitable lunge and bites from Demi. I took to wearing thick socks in the hope that his teeth would not be able to penetrate through. That evil look I saw at the shelter the day he was adopted continued to haunt me. I was sure he was the meanest cat on earth, maybe even possessed.

"What do you see in this cat?" I continued to ask Laurie and Barry. But they assured me he wasn't like this with them, that he was as loving and affectionate a cat as they could ever hope for.

The years went by, and Laurie and Barry had their first child, Karen. Up until then, Demi had Laurie and Barry all to himself. Now a sweet, new baby was threatening his superior status in the home. He was jealous, and he was angry. He scratched Karen several times and could not be trusted to be near her. A phone call to me and I was asked to declaw him. Sweet revenge? I thought I would feel somewhat vindicated, but it was a thankless task and one, in spite of my dislike for Demi, I hated to do. If he didn't have reason to hate me before, he certainly did now. Were we to remain mortal enemies for life?

Demi's woes didn't end there. He began to vomit on a daily basis. I diagnosed him with irritable bowel syndrome and recommended he be put on daily prednisone to control the irritation that was causing the chronic vomiting. The medication was very successful in controlling the vomiting, but it also left him crankier than ever. Demi was his own worst enemy. If only he could control his temper, I thought, he would be so much happier. If there was such a thing as anger management for cats, I would have suggested Demi be the first to sign up.

Three years later, Laurie and Barry had their second child, a son this time, whom they named Gregory. Everyone held their breath to see what antic, what drama would be the next chapter in Demi's life. But the years mellowed Demi, and not much happened as he went into old age. He may have even slowed down with his ankle attacking, but I never stopped flinching when I entered their home. I decided Demi was going to live a very, very long cat life mostly because he was just too mean a cat to ever die.

One day, when Demi reached his sixteenth year of life, Laurie called to tell me Demi was sick. She was very worried about him. He had stopped eating; he wasn't drinking either and was just moping around, not moving much. I told her to drive him up to my office right away. Because he was so mean, it had always been next to impossible for me to examine him without heavy sedation. He had that "do not touch me or I will kill you" look, which kept me fearful and respectful of him always. So it was with a certain amount of dread that I awaited for their arrival. When Laurie arrived and pulled Demi out of his carrier, I could see right away he was very sick. He didn't hiss at me, lunge at me, or try to take my eyes out when I examined him. The mere fact that I could touch him at all was a sign that he was very ill. I was even able to draw blood from him, something he was able to get from me with ease, but never me from him.

The blood test revealed end-stage kidney failure. There was nothing I could do for him. From the day I met this feisty kitten, I had teased Laurie and Barry that the final task of putting Demi down would be my pleasure, my ultimate revenge. But that wasn't the case at all. In fact, what I felt was just the opposite. I realized a lot of things at that moment. I realized that Demi didn't have half a brain as Barry often teased, but a rather complex one. I realized that in some strange way I enjoyed our adversarial relationship and that relationships are always more complex than you think they are. I realized that I liked this cat after all. Demi was a black-and-white cat, but he was filled with shades of gray, like all of us. Mostly, I finally saw what Laurie and Barry had seen in him all those years: there would never be another cat like Demi; and after all, I would miss him too.

Demi

Sekhmet, the Twin Sister of Bastet

Less famous than her sister, Sekhmet had a darker side. She was also a goddess and was depicted as a woman with the head of a lion. She represented the darker, negative side of the goddess. Sekhmet symbolized the destructive forces in nature as well as in human nature. Bastet was everything pure and good. Together, the sister goddesses were a balance of good and evil.

The African Serval

It was a call I never expected to get. Although I have an exclusive feline practice, I do occasionally get calls to see other species of animals. I have gotten calls on dogs, of course, but also hamsters, guinea pigs, birds, ducks, lizards, and even a snake. But when I got a call from a woman in New Hampshire to ask if I would see her African serval, even though it is technically a cat, I was completely taken aback.

An African serval is truly a wildcat. It can be seen in parts of Africa and in zoos. The female can weigh up to forty pounds and the male up to fifty-five pounds. Its life expectancy is twelve to twenty years, which these days is very similar to the domestic cat's. It is a slender animal with long legs, a smallish head, and a relatively short tail. It has oval ears that are set close together and a very distinctive spotted pattern on its body. Clearly, it is not a cute little domestic kitty cat. So why was a woman calling me from another state wanting to know if I would treat her serval?

I quickly picked up the phone. A young woman introduced herself as Debbie and politely asked me if I would see her serval, Akilah. She was in a desperate situation, and without immediate care, she was certain her serval would die. She went on to tell me that these cats are prone to eating inanimate objects, which she was afraid the cat had done. She was vomiting up everything she tried to eat, including plain water. I asked her why she called me. Weren't there veterinarians closer to where she lived? It would take her about four hours by car to get to my clinic, so it didn't make sense to me. She then confessed that she was afraid to take the serval locally. In New Hampshire, it is illegal to keep a wildcat in your home without a special permit, which she did not have. If she brought the cat there, she was sure they would confiscate Akilah. She'd heard about me through a mutual friend who bred Bengals and was a client of mine here in Connecticut.

I was faced with several ethical dilemmas. Firstly, was it legal for me to see and treat a serval? Was I obligated to tell the state that I had a wildcat in the office? To whom was my obligation—to the law or to a sick cat in need of immediate medical attention?

I decided that as a practicing veterinarian, my obligation was to the health and well-being of the cat. I would first do what I could for the cat and worry about the legal aspect later. Of course, there were practical things to consider. I had my staff to worry about. How aggressive was this cat? How would I handle a wild animal? After all, I wasn't a zoo veterinarian and didn't have the proper restraints necessary for the occasion. Debbie assured me that if she were there to hold her cat, nobody would get hurt. Akilah was very well behaved, and she had complete control over her. As long as she was there, we had little to fear. I told her get in her car and come over as soon as she could.

I alerted the staff. Linda was beside herself with excitement. She absolutely loves "big" cats, and I have to admit, so do I. Four hours later, Debbie showed up with the serval. We all knew she was going to be a big cat, but when she came in to the building, she took our breath away. One look and we all agreed we couldn't let this cat die due to her ownership being illegal. She was magnificent and clearly very much loved.

Her owner held on tight as I injected her with a tranquilizer. Within minutes, she was feeling sleepy. We prepped her for surgery and moved her to the operating room where I began my abdominal exploratory to look for the foreign object blocking her intestinal tract. There are many, many feet of small intestines, and I had to start from the beginning and work my way through every inch of it. I finally found the offending object about halfway down the intestinal tract. The intestines were inflamed and swollen where the object was, ready to rupture. If this had happened, the serval would be dead in hours. She was probably a day or so away from death.

I put Akilah in Linda's capable hands during her post-op recovery and went out to tell Debbie that all went well in the OR. What I had removed was a thick piece of rubber, thick enough to completely obstruct the cat. When she thought about it, she realized that a very large piece of rubber was missing from her stationary bike's handlebar. She broke out crying with relief. She loved her Akilah so much; she would have been devastated if she had lost her. This cat slept with her and her husband every night, and although people were respectfully afraid of her, the family cherished her as an equal family member.

That night, I brought Debbie and Akilah home with me. Normally, a surgery of this type would require an overnight stay at the clinic, but I had no place to keep a cat of this size. Besides, the owner wanted to be with her through the night. No hotel would take this pair in. My home was the only logical place for them to stay. I didn't tell my husband, the attorney. I thought it better to simply surprise him.

When my husband came home, he found a strange woman sitting on our living room sofa and a sign on one of the bedroom doors that said, Do Not Enter: Serval Inside. When he looked at me with his very perplexed look, a look I have become very familiar with, I reminded him that he married a veterinarian. We all took turns checking on Akilah, in fact arguing whose turn it was. My Cornish Rex, Paco, tried to sneak in to take a look too. I quickly discouraged that potentially foolish act.

The next morning, the serval was 100 percent better. Lively, alert, and ready to eat. The owner thanked me over and over as we said our good-byes. I still question if I did the right thing by not turning them in, but I followed my heart and ultimately felt good about it. I never thought I would hear from them again.

Two years later, almost to the day, Debbie called again. Akilah had eaten something yet again and was showing all the same signs of being obstructed. I shook my head in disbelief as I faced my ethical dilemma for a second time.

"Come right over," I said. I couldn't let them down. For better or for worse, I was not going to let this serval die, not on my watch.

The second surgery went as well as the first. This time, she had swallowed the major part of a tennis ball, another rubber object. Akilah recovered so quickly that we didn't even need a sleepover. I think my husband was a little bit disappointed that he didn't get to see the serval again. The attorney in him, however, still pointed the finger at me, questioning my decision to re-treat this cat.

In general, I do not believe that wild animals should be kept in homes as pets. But given the choice between saving the life of an animal and abiding by the law, I think I would do what I did for Akilah again and again.

As Debbie left with Akilah for the second time, I warned her to please keep Akilah away from all rubber objects because the third time, she may not be so lucky. Then I looked at my staff and reminded them that what happens at the Complete Cat Clinic stays at the Complete Cat Clinic.

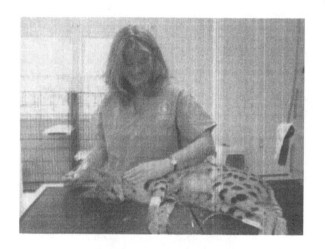

Dr. Eisen and Akilah

Linda and Akilah

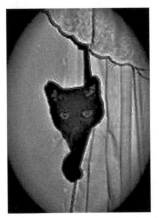

Descendants of Cats

All cats are a descendant of the *Felis sylvestris* species, which is divided into the African wildcat, European wildcat, and Steppe wildcat. The smallest of the descendants is a rusty spotted cat from Sri Lanka. Weighing in at about four pounds, it is half the size of the domestic cat. The largest descendant is the tiger, with the male Siberian weighing up to 660 pounds. The lion is not just the king of the jungle; he is the king of all cats. It is the only feline that lives in organized social groups. The fastest cat is the cheetah, which is also the fastest land animal. It can go up to sixty miles per hour over short distances. Unlike other big cats, it does not roar, but, like your domestic kitty, it does purr.

For humans, a fingerprint is a unique characteristic of who we are; for the feline, their tabby patterned marking is what makes them unique from each other.

Joey and Charlie

Joey is my first cousin, and he is and will always be exactly one year and six days younger than me. When we were growing up, I somehow thought he would catch up and surpass me to become older. Maybe I was counting in dog or cat years, expecting him to age more quickly than his human counterparts. But of course, that never happened. Having fathers who are brothers, it was not surprising that we would have a lot in common. Joey and I did everything together in our childhood, and in many ways, we were much like our dads. But in one important way, we were always different.

Joey never wanted a pet. He never had one growing up, except for a fish, which he says doesn't count. He never felt the painful pangs that some children feel toward wanting a pet. I, on the other hand, ached and begged for any furry four-legged creature I could keep in the house. But our parents had the old European belief that all animals were wild and belonged outdoors, especially cats. My grandmother once discovered a stray cat in the house and quickly got out the broom, screaming in Yiddish, "Aroys mit dem katz!" (Out with you, cat!) Since I couldn't have a pet, in our childhood games, I pretended to be a dog. If I couldn't have a dog or a cat, I could at least pretend to be one. At the time, it seemed perfectly normal to be an animal, walk around on all fours and bark or meow. Joey refused to be an animal and so remained in human form.

We are both much older now, and Joey still isn't a cat lover. But he now appreciates the feline in a way he never did growing up, all thanks to one cat that fortuitously and surprisingly came into his life.

It all started because Joey desperately wanted a particular apartment on Barnes Avenue in the Bronx, where his friends Lenny and Linda were living. He loved the location and the layout and told them that if they ever moved out, he wanted to live there. His friends had a cat named Charlie, whom they had found in the neighborhood. Charlie was a big, handsome black-and-white tuxedo cat that ruled the streets of the Bronx neighborhood where he lived. Everyone knew him on the street and respected him. He could often be found lying in the middle of a city street, stretched out looking like he didn't want to be anyplace else but right there. If a car came, he would simply rise, slowly and deliberately stretch some more, and meander over to the sidewalk. He walked with a confidence and a swagger that said, "All right, I'll get up this time, but don't ask me to do it again."

One time, Charlie didn't get up quickly enough and got hit by a car. His leg was badly broken and required surgery that would cost $450, a sum that at the time was astronomical for two young hippies living off a song and a prayer. Somehow, the money was scraped together, and they were able to pay for the surgery Charlie needed. Charlie never made that mistake again, but it left him with a distaste of car rides that would haunt him and Joey forever.

When Charlie was about a year and a half old, his owners decided to move to an apartment in Hoboken, New Jersey. The new apartment didn't allow pets. They offered Joey the apartment, and he ecstatically said yes. What they didn't immediately tell him was that there was a condition. They also didn't divulge the condition until the very day they were moving out and Joey was moving in. The apartment came with Charlie. Not only did Joey never want a cat, he had never taken care of another living creature in his life (except for the fish, which, as often happens with fish, died).

"I didn't want him," he told me. "I didn't even like cats." But he wanted the apartment so badly that he agreed to make Charlie his responsibility. Besides, he had no choice; he had already abandoned his other prospects, and his furniture was on the moving van. Little did he know that it would be the beginning of a twelve-year relationship that would not only outlast his first marriage, but would also be one of the most memorable and loving relationships of his life.

He may not have been able to help pay the rent, but in every other way, Charlie turned out to be a perfect roommate. He was affectionate, loyal, and smart. When Joey came home and called for him, he always came running home. Always. He would put his big paws around Joey and hug him. He also drooled profusely when he was happy, so hugs were always accompanied with a big wet spot. But getting soaked with his slobbery drool was a small price to pay for his affection. The wet spot became a sign you'd been hugged by Charlie.

Joey describes Charlie as a big, handsome hunk of a cat. He had charisma, good looks, manners, and intelligence. Everyone loved him, just everyone. When he sauntered into a room, he was a presence that could not be ignored. Was he everything Joey wanted to be? If he were human, no woman could resist him. Many people thought of him as more doglike than catlike. If he understood what they were thinking, he might have been insulted. After all, he was the quintessential cat and stood for everything feline, except perhaps the drooling.

Over the next twelve years, Joey moved twelve times. With every move, his major consideration was Charlie. It had to be a place, generally on the ground level, that Charlie could get in and out of the house from. There was one apartment on the second floor, but Charlie was able to climb out a window and walk down a flight of stairs to the outside. With each move, he settled in almost instantly. He learned his way around the neighborhood and adjusted to each new home with ease. He was remarkable in his ability to adapt to every new situation.

Once the furniture had been moved to the new home, it was time to move Charlie. Every car ride with him was a nightmarish ordeal resembling an exorcism. He never forgot the car that left him with the hardware that held his leg together. Inevitably, vomiting and endless screaming accompanied each trip. But all was forgotten and forgiven once he was at the new house. Joey and Charlie would settle in together just like two best buds.

I asked Cousin Joey why he moved so often. "Well, I moved when the year's lease ran out, I guess," he said. I think he just had wanderlust. Joey and Charlie were like two bachelors setting up their pad in each home, looking for adventure, occasionally getting into trouble, but always managing to survive. When Joey dated, the women had to pass the Charlie test. When he brought his date home and they didn't like Charlie, there was no second date.

Before Joey sat down to eat, he always placed a bowl of fresh food out for Charlie. They ate together, sat on the couch to watch TV together, and drifted off to sleep together. He was the ideal roommate in every respect, and with every move and every passing year, they loved each other more and more.

The last place Joey moved to with Charlie was in Bethel, Connecticut. It was there that he helped Joey get through a failed marriage. When his wife wanted to take Charlie in the divorce agreement, Joey put his foot down. She could have the car, the artwork, whatever she wanted, but there was no way Charlie was leaving the house. Joey and Charlie had become inseparable. The wife finally relented, moved on, and the two of them went back to being just two bachelors in the house.

Charlie had never been sick a day in his life, but at the age of fourteen, he suddenly became very ill. Because he hated to travel in the car, Joey found a veterinarian that would come to the house. I was not living in the area at the time and couldn't be the one to take care of Charlie, but we conferred often over long-distance phone calls, going over blood work, discussing treatment options. Sadly, Charlie was diagnosed with terminal liver cancer. Nothing could be done for him. I wanted to be there with Joey. I thought I could help him get through this. I wanted to make him laugh like we made each other laugh as children, but it was a journey Joey and Charlie had to go through on their own. Sadly and profoundly, Charlie died in Joey's arms where he drifted off to sleep for the last time. Now it was Joey who wrapped his arms around Charlie, and it was Joey who left the wet spot on Charlie with his tears.

Joey spent the next four hours constructing a little coffin for Charlie. He went to his woodworking studio and painstakingly built a beautiful box from white pine. He constructed the coffin with rabbet joints, which not only made the process more time-consuming, but also made the coffin more durable. Together with his close friend Harvey, he spent the rest of the day digging the grave. He chose a location behind the house in Bethel, in the woods where Charlie spent his final years chasing rabbits, hunting moles, and climbing trees. No more horrible car rides for Charlie, not even in the afterlife.

Joey has since happily remarried, and he and his wife just celebrated their sixteenth wedding anniversary. He never got another cat and doesn't want one. He fell in love with Charlie, who taught him the qualities that a cat can possess, but doesn't feel the need for another cat. Maybe, if a cat like Charlie falls into his life the way Charlie did, he will have another cat; but he isn't sure there will ever be another cat like Charlie, not for Joey. They were best buddies until the end.

"I feel truly blessed to have had Charlie in my life," Joey smiles. "Yes, lucky and blessed."

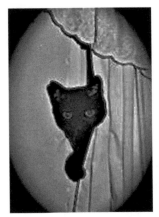

Garfield

On June 19, 1978, cartoonist Jim Davis created one of the most iconic cats of contemporary culture. Obnoxious, fat, lazy, and lasagna-loving Garfield eased his way into everyone's heart, young and old alike. Although Garfield was often mean to Jon and abusive to Odie, people grew to love his irascible nature.

Perhaps the reason we love him so much is that he shares many of our likes and dislikes. However, he is free to express them while we must remain civilized. Garfield hated Mondays, hated the vet's office, and took great pride in annoying Jon and Odie whenever he had the chance.

The *Garfield* franchise continues to be hugely popular as well and an enormous financial success.

The Cat Lady of Boboli Gardens

I almost didn't see her.

What first caught my eye was a rather large gray tabby cat eating a big piece of white chicken meat. On my trips, I love to take pictures of cats that I see in other parts of the world. I have pictures of cats lounging on French windowsills, sunbathing on Grecian sidewalks, hiding behind a Scottish boulder. My photo albums are filled with pictures of these cats, and when I look back at them, they help me to remember exactly where I was when the photo was taken.

This time my husband and I were on a trip to Florence, Italy. We decided to spend a day strolling through the Boboli Gardens, which extend from the hill behind the Pitti Palace and comprise an area of eleven acres. Once home to the Medici family, this majestic palace, together with the gardens, are steeped in history, art, and culture. Open to the public, the gardens are an outdoor museum of Roman sculpture and sixteenth—and seventeenth-century works. Millions of tourists from all over the world come to visit the gardens, and in 2008, I was one of them. It was there that I spotted this gray tabby cat.

What first struck me about the cat in the Boboli Gardens was how fat and healthy he looked. Usually the cats I see in other countries are skinny, scrawny creatures living off hunting and the scraps they might find behind restaurants and in garbage cans. I aimed my camera at him, getting ready to take his picture, when I heard, "Suzy, vieni qui, mangia, Tommy, anche tu, mangia, mangia, vieni" (Suzy, come here, eat, Tommy, you too, eat, eat, come).

That was when I looked up and saw her. She could have been forty years old. She could have been sixty. She was wearing very plain clothes, jeans with neutral colors, browns and tans. She had a large, plain backpack from which she was taking out food and arranging it in neat piles for the cats. Nothing about her stood out. She wasn't hiding the fact that she was feeding these cats, but I didn't think she particularly wanted to be noticed either. There were three cats in this little group, and she appeared to have named them all. There was Suzy, a calico; Tommy, the gray tabby that I first noticed; and Timmy, a big, handsome redhead. All were well nourished (perhaps too much so), and all were busily eating what this woman was dishing out from her pack.

I stood there for about ten minutes simply watching the interaction between this woman and these cats. I was completely mesmerized as I observed her not only feed them, but also give them all a looking over as they approached the food. She looked in their ears, opened their mouths quickly to check teeth, ran her fingers through their fur. Being a veterinarian, I know the routine of a physical, and she was clearly doing that with each and every one of them. Had she gone to veterinary school? I wondered.

I had to talk to this woman. I had so much I wanted to know. My Italian was a bit rusty, but I began, "Buon giorno, questi gatti, abitano nel giardino?" (Good day, do these cats live in the gardens?)

"Si, si," she said.

I continued, "Ci sono altri gatti che abitano nel giardino?" (Are there other cats living here too?)

Again she replied, "Si, si."

"Quanti ci sono?" (How many are there?) I asked.

She told me there were fifty-five cats presently living in the gardens. She went on to tell me that there used to be 250 of them when she first started to care for them. Cats have been living in the gardens for hundreds of years, she said, and most if not all of them were born here.

"Ma lei, viene ogni giorno con cibo per i gatti?" (Did she come to feed them every day?) I asked.

"Si, vengo ogni giorno," (Yes, I come every day) she replied.

Where did she get the food? I asked. She got the food from restaurants, from anywhere and everywhere food was being thrown out or not used. She never stopped feeding the cats as we spoke, never stopped attending to them.

Where were the others? I asked. Where were the other fifty-two cats? She told me they were scattered throughout the gardens in small groups. Did she know where they all were?

"Ma, certamente," (Well, certainly) she said.

And had she named them all? Of course, she had named them all. She knew each and every cat and exactly where they could be found in the park.

I know doctors, lawyers, accountants, and nurses, and I have enormous respect for all these people who have successful careers; but as I stood and watched this woman, I had as much admiration for her at that moment as any of them. She had devoted her life to taking care of the cats in the Boboli Gardens of Florence, Italy.

My husband, pulling on my arm, said it was time to move on. We had much we wanted to see, the gardens were very large, and we had only one day in which to explore this fabulous place. I took my photograph of the cat, whom I now knew as Tommy, and reluctantly walked away, continuing our walk through the gardens. We walked past the sculpture of Neptune rising above the *isolotto*, the amphitheatre, the Grotta di Buontalenti. Everything was incredibly beautiful, with a rich history and an aesthetic that was well worth the price of admission. People from all over the world travel and spend thousands of dollars to visit Florence. They consider it a privilege to spend one day, perhaps two, in the gardens.

As we continued our stroll, it struck me that these cats actually *live* in the Boboli Gardens. Usually I feel a little sorry for the cats I see that live on the streets. They have that hungry, tired look, the look of a hard life, but not these cats. They live in one of the most beautiful places on earth. And not only that, they have a dedicated personal servant! She collects food for them, knows where they are, and delivers it to them in already cut-up bite-size chunks. She checks them over daily, and if they are not well, I am sure they are attended to. I am certain that they are all healthy. There are no cars in the park, no pollution to speak of, fresh water everywhere, flowers, birds, trees. The Boboli Gardens are truly heaven on earth. People no longer live in the Pitti Palace and haven't for many, many years. But the cats live here. They are now the royalty of the Pitti Palace.

We continued walking, and my thoughts turned to this woman. Did she have a family? How does a person come to do such a thing? Why did she dedicate her life to these cats? She clearly didn't want to be noticed; she was almost in the shadows. She knew how to hide. She knew how to scrounge for food. Was she homeless herself? Did she find a place tucked away somewhere in the gardens where she herself lived and nobody knew? I wanted to go back and ask her all these questions. I found myself wanting to know all about her. She was the most fascinating person I had met on this trip. Perhaps a part of me related to her. After all, I have also dedicated my life to the care of cats, only I did it by opening a cat hospital. In that way, I realized we were kindred spirits.

After walking for several hours, I once again heard her voice.

"Gianni, Patricia, Paolo, vieni qui, mangia, mangia, vieni a mangiare subito!" (Johnny, Patricia, Paul, come here, eat, eat, come quickly to eat!)

I turned to look, and there she was, dishing out more food to another group of happy, well-fed, and clearly well-loved cats. They were surrounding her, enjoying the afternoon sun, enjoying an Italian feast. She petted each and every one, and like the cats themselves, she seemed completely happy to be doing just this and nothing more. I would have loved to ask her about her life and how she came to be taking care of these cats, but I felt that it would be an intrusion. Although she was willing enough to talk about the cats, she seemed to prefer to remain "in the shadows."

Later that day, after we left the Boboli Gardens and headed back to the apartment we were staying in, I came across a poster for a missing leopard. I saw this same poster all over Florence, plastered on walls and on the windshields of cars. His name was Leo, and he was a beautiful very big spotted leopard. I couldn't believe someone was actually keeping a wild full-size leopard in an apartment. No wonder he ran off, I thought; leopards are not meant to live in apartments.

Missing!

Then I had another thought. Where would a full-size leopard go to hide? Where would he go to get away from being held in captivity, where there is no traffic, where there are plenty of trees and grass and water, where he can find food and have a perfect place to hide? He would go to the Boboli Gardens, of course! And I would bet anything that the cat lady knows exactly where he is, and she will *never ever* give his secret hiding place away.

The cat lady and Tommy

Acknowledgements

We want to thank those who helped us write this book. First and foremost, and with deepest gratitude, we thank the people who shared their stories. We know that some of the stories were hard to revisit because they brought back painful memories but they shared them anyway. We also want to thank Peter Riggs, Dr. Eisen's husband, who worked countless hours helping us to edit the book and to stay focused. Thanks to John Francese, Linda's husband, for his never-ending support no matter what new project she may come up with, he always lets her follow her dreams. To Cilka Castro and Johnny Francese for their love of cats and for inspiring us to go forward. Special thanks to Greg Francese, for being our GPS so that we never get lost and for just being who he is. Thanks to Linda's parents, Lino and Vittoria Pasqualone who, even though they are not the animals lovers that Linda is, showed her a sense of love and generosity for all living things. It is with their nurturing, principles and foundation that she was able to open her heart and have compassion and understanding for all beautiful creatures, furry or not. Last but not least, where would we be without some of our dear friends and family who gave us invaluable feedback on our stories: Carmella Smagula, Barbara Ahern, Jerilyn Fisher, Carol Pasqualone, Christina Pasqualone, Linda Eisen, Nina Francese, and Christine Addiego. Thanks to Dr. Eisen's parents, Henry and Florence Eisen, without who's help she could never have become a veterinarian. They also taught her how to be a compassionate and giving person, qualities that helped her see these stories in people and cats.

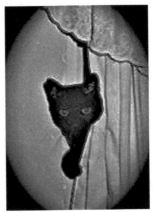

About the Authors

Dr. Sharon Eisen has been a practicing veterinarian since 1984. In 1991, she realized her dream of opening a feline-only practice in Brookfield, Connecticut. The Complete Cat Clinic was the very first cats-only hospital in the state.

While owning and operating the clinic, Dr. Eisen has also been breeding cats for the past fifteen years. Some of her cats have appeared on television and have been top-ranking show cats with many ribbons to their credit; and others have simply been beautiful and treasured companions.

In addition to devoting her career to the care and well-being of cats, Dr. Eisen has an abiding interest in the human-animal connection. She has conducted programs in elementary schools to teach students about pet care. She has led pet bereavement groups, and she has brought cats and dogs to nursing homes to serve as pet therapists.

For many years, Dr. Eisen has wanted to share these wonderful and compelling stories. The time has finally come.

Dr. Eisen lives in Danbury, Connecticut, with her husband and four cats: Paco, Hershey, Paulie Newman, and Rosie.

Linda Francese fulfilled a lifelong dream in 2004 and began working with cats as the head technician at the Complete Cat Veterinary Clinic in Brookfield, Connecticut. A year later, she joined Dr. Eisen as co-owner of the Plaid Plus Cattery, breeding British Shorthair cats.

Earlier in her career, Mrs. Francese worked in radio for more than twenty years. In addition to becoming well-known as an on-air personality, she did commercial copywriting, voice-overs, and radio production at numerous New York area radio stations, including WHUD 100.7 FM. During that time, Mrs. Francese was nominated for many awards and, in 1998, won the prestigious New York State Broadcasters Award for outstanding commercial.

Mrs. Francese lives in Brookfield with her husband, two sons, and five cats: TiVo, Rhiannon, A-Rod, Jovi, and the latest addition, Wolf Blitzer.

How did you come up for the idea of the book?

Linda: After working together, we found that we were a pretty good team. We started a blog and then a podcast. There was still so much that we wanted to share with as many people as we could. So one cold Sunday afternoon, we sat down together and tried to figure out how to do this. Sharon came up with the idea after remembering reading a book where people were being interviewed and these stories were being archived. As you probably have already guessed, we believe that every cat has a story, and we've heard hundreds of them from everyone that walks into the clinic. We thought that sharing these stories in book form would be the greatest way to pay tribute to these special relationships.

What's your favorite story and why?

Linda: My favorite story is Greg and TiVo. Not because I wrote it, not because Greg is my son and TiVo is my cat, but because I feel it shares something that has touched everyone's life—autism. Everyone knows someone with autism, and this story brings some awareness to it. It also offers hope and hopefully good feelings. Looking back, I feel that the story itself is too short, that I should have gone deeper into my own feelings. But autism is not an easy thing to accept, and at the time that I wrote the story, that was as deep as I could get. I could go deeper now. You come to accept it more and more as time goes on, and you see what your child can do and are truly amazed by him. It still is not easy, but it's so much better. I know that Greg can do anything. I hope that the story can inspire or help someone that is at the same level that I was when I wrote it. However, I'd also want them to know something that Greg's nursery school teacher told me: "He'll only get better. He'll never get worse," and it's true. I don't think that I could be any prouder of him.

Dr. Eisen: For me it's "The Cat Lady of Boboli Gardens." I was in one of my favorite places on earth, Florence, Italy. The weather was spectacular, and this woman totally intrigued me. It was also a story I had to be a bit more creative with as I couldn't interview her, like so many of the other stories in the book. I loved watching her take care of these cats, and knowing that she didn't do it for money or recognition made her all the more attractive to me. She was like St. Francis, and I loved her for that.

Why did you give up radio to work with cats?

Linda: I have always been a cat person, but I felt that going into the veterinary field would be difficult for me. There is a lot of heartache when a cat is sick or when there is a euthanasia. I didn't think that I could handle it. Radio was another passion that I had. It's what I hold a degree in. However, I grew up when disc jockeys could actually talk about the music, and that's what I wanted to do. I didn't want to play the same songs over and over again and read from a card. I wanted to be a radio personality, which I was for many years. However, radio has changed, and I became very disenchanted. When we moved to Connecticut and I saw a job opening at the Complete Cat for a veterinary technician, I thought, why not? I didn't have any experience, but I had a cat, and I had the passion to be the best that I could be. I walked into the clinic for my interview only to be greeted by Bentley and Violet, the king and queen of the Complete Cat. Well, Sharon didn't hire me. She hired someone with more experience. I couldn't blame her, I would have done the same thing, but I was really heartbroken. I looked at other veterinary technician openings, but I wanted to work at Sharon's place. Something was telling me that I had to work there. A month later, Sharon had a position as a receptionist open, and she called me. I eagerly took it. I had to be there. A few months after that, the veterinary technician position opened up, and the rest is history.

Why did you open a cats-only hospital?

Dr. Eisen: Before I graduated veterinary school, I was living on Long Island and would drive by an exclusive feline practice on my way home. One day, I stopped in, and it was fantastic. That hospital was one of the first feline-only practices in the country, and I loved the atmosphere it provided for the patients. At that point, my dream was to do the same wherever I settled down. It turned out to be Danbury, Connecticut, and in 1991, my dream became a reality. Don't misunderstand. I love all creatures, but cats are my passion, and I wanted to give them a space of their own. The Complete Cat Clinic was the first cats-only hospital in the state, and I am very proud of what we have created here.

What impact do you hope this book will have on its readers?

Linda: People come in all the time and say, "I know you'll think I'm crazy, but my cats are like my children to me." I don't think they're crazy. I know the feeling. Some will even say, "I don't have children, so my cats are my children," and I say to them, "I have children, and my cats are still my babies." I want people to know that it's OK to love a cat. Cats are special, and certain cats are extra special (just like Beta to me and Bentley to Sharon). As I sit here and write this, A-Rod is all curled up next to me. I can always count on him to be there for me, to love me, and to bump me when I need to be bumped! It's not crazy to love a cat. It's crazy not to. You don't know what you're missing.

Dr. Eisen: I wanted to honor the relationships between cats and people. These stories are really odes to them, and my hope is that people will be able to relate to these stories and know that they are not alone in what they have felt for their feline companions.

Where do you get your stories?

Linda: Every day, and I mean every day, someone comes to the clinic and will tell us all about their cat. This just proves how important this creature is in their lives. When someone tells us the story of their cat, there is actually a glow on their face and a smile on their lips. It's not hard to come by a love story about a cat in this business.

Dr. Eisen: We also get them outside of the office. I've heard stories at the bank, at the post office, at the mall, really almost anywhere and everywhere, even on a street corner in Seattle.

Were people forthcoming in telling their stories, and if not, why?

Linda: Most people were forthcoming. It wasn't hard at all to hear all about their cat and why they were so special. We tried to find the most compelling part of their cat story to put into the book because, let's face it, every cat really has more than one story. Some, though, were hard. As in the case of a very dear friend of ours. She thought she was ready to talk about her beloved cat that had passed away. We were all ready for the interview. She came in, and her emotions just took over. She apologized over and over, but the tears were coming from such a deep, deep place in her heart that she had buried far down two years ago. She was just not ready to tell the story. It was still just way too raw for her. Someday, she will be ready to tell her story and relish the good times. Maybe in the next book!

Were some stories harder to write than others?

Linda: Without a doubt! Some stories came flying out. I witnessed Sharon write "The Lady of the Boboli Gardens" in about three seconds! Then there were some that felt like pulling teeth out. We would say, "I know there is a story in here, I just know it." I can't even count how many times certain stories were written, rewritten, and then rewritten again. We wanted to bring you the best we could. I hope that we succeeded.

How do you feel about the notion that people don't bring their cats in for veterinary care as often as they should?

Dr. Eisen: The data is out there that more dog owners bring their dogs in than cat owners. I'm not sure why that is, but maybe people believe that because cats are so much more independent than dogs that they can take care of themselves. Of course, that isn't true. Cats need medical care and preventative care every bit as much as dogs do, and I hope that someday, we see more of this happening in the world.

Are there more stories to come?

Dr. Eisen: You bet. I hope this is only the beginning. I want to keep this a tradition and be able to honor cats every year that are or were special in people's lives. I want people to continue to share their stories with us, and hopefully next year and the year after that, more of our most memorable felines will have their stories told.

Do you have a way for people to share those stories with you?

Dr. Eisen: Yes, they can write them to us at our Web site, and we'll try to write it up and include it in *Cat Tales Volume Two*.

www.cattalesbook.com

Hope to hear from you all!

Index